GOD
SPEAKS
— •—IN—• —
TROUBLED TIMES
SERMONS OF
ENCOURAGEMENT

DR. EARL PETERSON, JR.

Book Cover Design: Prize Publishing House

Printed by: Prize Publishing House, LLC in the United States of America.

First printing edition 2021.

Prize Publishing House

P.O. Box 9856 Chesapeake, VA 23321

www.PrizePublishingHouse.com

ISBN (Paperback): 978-1-7364457-6-1

ISBN (E-Book): 978-1-7364457-7-8

Library of Congress Control Number: 2021906484

CONTENTS

ACKNOWLEDGMENTS

I give special thanks to the love of my life, friend, and confidant, Bettie Peterson - my wife of over 46 years, for her continual faithful, prayerful support of me in the ministry and her unconditional love.

I thank my three daughters, Takeitha, Andrea, Krystina, and their husbands, Vincent, Larry, and Tracy, for always being supportive and at my every call. I appreciate my oldest daughter, Takeitha, who strongly encouraged me to publish this book of sermons. Additionally, I appreciate my nephew, Pastor Eric Williams and my daughters Andrea and Takeitha, and my adopted daughter, Merica Green, who are all published authors, who motivated me weekly to achieve this publishing goal. Thank you to my sisters, Jo Ann and Marie, and my brother, James, for always encouraging me in doing the Lord's work.

I defer to my many mentors down through the years, of whom I stand on their shoulders and give humble reverence: the late Bishops Young, Moody, Johnson, Dunn, J. W. White, and so many others who are now considered the great cloud of witnesses. I also appreciate Bishop Roy L. H. Winbush, whom I have admired down through the years. Thank you to my many Pastors: the late Superintendents A. L. Mack, E. M. Green, Elders Clifton Roberts, and Walker, and my former Pastor, Superintendent Maurice Johnson, who is still serving in Leesville, LA, along with many, many others. I give special thanks to the Women of God, Mothers, Missionaries, Evangelists, and Prayer Warriors, who have always put their arms around me and taught me to pray and seek the face of God, shaping my life of prayer, praise, and genuine love for my family. Thank God for the Church Of God In Christ.

I am grateful for the three churches that I was privileged to Pastor while serving in the United States Army: Northern Germany Church Of God In Christ (COGIC) in Osterholtz-Sharmbeck/Bremerhaven, Germany; Free For All COGIC in Darmstadt, Germany; and the Bountiful Blessings COGIC in Colorado Springs, Colorado, where I am presently privileged to serve, who allowed and is allowing me to lead them and preach God's Word regularly.

Lastly, I must mention my praying Mother, the late Nazarene Hearne Peterson, and my Dad, the late Superintendent Earl Peterson, Sr., for training me to be a man of integrity and a man who understands, honors, and respects authority.

DEDICATION

I take this privilege to dedicate this book, my first publication, to my loving and darling wife, Jurisdictional Supervisor (Colorado Jurisdiction Church Of God In Christ), Mother Bettie Faye Elbert Peterson; to the Bountiful Blessings Church Of God In Christ in Colorado Springs, CO; to every military family, active and retired; and to my parents, the late Superintendent Earl Peterson, Sr. and the late Nazarene Hearne Peterson. This book of sermons is also dedicated to my precious grandchildren: Trachelle; Madisyn; Kyler; and Zhane', who will one day carry the torch of ministry legacy.

FOREWORD

March 2020 ushered in an era of impossibilities and uncertainties that have plagued society since that time. Financial woes, untimely deaths, and school shutdowns created a domino effect of widespread panic. Although we are still grappling with the complexities of the pandemic, there is still hope through the preached Word of God.

Dr. Earl Peterson, Jr. has captured a collection of life-giving, mental shifting, and faith-building messages to transform one's life from breakdown to breakthrough. Position yourself to catapult into a new frame of thinking as you peruse through this timely book. Turn the pandemic into a PLANdemic. Plan to prosper, heal, and grow as a result of this power-packed book.

Dr. Eric Allen Williams

Author, Demon Choir - Overcoming the Voice of Fear

CHAPTER 1

By My Spirit Saith The Lord of Hosts

Scripture Reference: Zechariah 4:1-14 KJV

This text comes from one of the Post Exilic prophets who was given the task of preaching to the children of Israel after they had been released from 70-year Babylonian captivity. Because they had been in bondage for so many years, one would think that just the sheer excitement of being released would spark an overwhelming spirit of joy, peace, and worship. But it did not work that way. Instead of a spirit of excitement, it seemed as if they gave way to a spirit of complacency, lackadaisicalness, uncaring, and laziness. They drifted into their world and forgot about what God required and wanted. So, in times when God's people are prone to resort to just sitting down doing nothing, we see God releasing a word through His prophets to whip us back into shape. God raised the prophet Zechariah and sent him to both the governor and high priest in the land.

Zerubbabel was the governor, and the high priest's name was Joshua. It was not Joshua, Moses' successor, but another man who bore the same name as that of Moses' minister.

1

Why did God send the prophet to Zerubbabel and Joshua? Zerubbabel had a job to do for God. His task was to ensure and supervise the rebuilding of the temple in Jerusalem. His mission, although a simple one, was much more than meets the eye. Several obstacles complicated his task of rebuilding the temple. First, the Jews were being released from Babylonian captivity and were in the midst of a significant resettling of life and property. Second, money and natural resources were scarce. Third, a major apathetic attitude had to be released and removed from the people's minds. And lastly, the people were also intimidated by the surrounding nations and were uncertain about the extent of their authority. These complications confronted Zerubbabel, but in many ways, these same problems confront God's people today.

When you start working for God, one source of sure encouragement is that you know that God called you to do the job. With that assurance, it is difficult, but without that knowledge, you will be tossed to and fro by the cunning craftiness of the devil. Knowing that God has commissioned you, sent you, and charged you will provide sufficient energy to counter the enemy's attacks and will be enough to challenge any opposer of the vision.

Zerubbabel, no doubt, was gifted and able to do God's bidding but was at this time feeling insufficient for the task at hand because of how things looked in the natural. Although things seem impossible, we must remember that we walk by faith and not by sight, and because of this, we can call those things that be not as though they were. Now, we must bear in mind that righteousness exalts a nation, but sin is a reproach to any people.

The prophet Zechariah, the messenger sent to encourage Zerubbabel, saw in a vision from God that Zerubbabel was the man for the job. Sometimes, it does not matter how gifted and talented we are; we sometimes feel insufficient for the task at hand. At this time, we must remember that *our sufficiency is of God (2 Corinthians 3:5, KJV)* and not of us or anyone else. We must not forget that it is God who grants and supplies all that is needed to accomplish whatever task He has laid upon us. *We can do all things through Christ who strengthens us (Philippians 4:13, KJV).*

So, do not allow the cares of life to intimidate you and cause you to lose out on the strength, power, and blessings of God. *Be strong in the Lord and the power of His might (Ephesians 6:10, KJV).* See to it that this old sinful world does not get the best of you. *You are a child of the most high God and will not be forced or led astray from the great things that God has in store for you (1 Corinthians 2:9, KJV).*

Psalm 37 reminds us to *trust in the Lord and do good, and you shall dwell in the land, and verily you shall be fed!!! (Psalm 37:3, KJV).* God sent Zechariah to Zerubbabel to encourage him, to give him good news from a far country. He was sent by God to strengthen his bowed-down head and to stir up the gift that was within him. There are mopers, complainers, grumblers, and whiners, but lift your heads, stop crying, and feeling sorry for yourself because God is your source and not your resource. You have to be confident and know that you are somebody special in God. Dry your weeping eyes, for God is on your side. Yes, God is on the side of the righteous. David said that *I have been young, and now I am old, but I have never seen the righteous forsaken, nor his seed begging for bread (Psalm 37:25, KJV).*

The foundation of God's house is dug deep into the earth and will not be shaken by the storms of life. *Be strong in the Lord and the power of His might (Ephesians 6:10, KJV).* Despite the enemy's desperate attempt to destroy the church, be rest assured that the church will not fail. Jesus said in Matthew 16:18, *upon this rock I will build my church, and the very gates (authority and power) of hell shall not prevail against it.* Now, your commitment to the cause of Christ will be tested daily, but *no temptation has taken you, but such as is common to man, but God will with the temptation provide a way of escape that you may be able to bear it.*

Zechariah's vision concerning the lampstand, olive trees, and the flow of the oil spoke to the fact that all of our accomplishments should be done in God's time and in God's way. The vision contained several characters in an order that spoke to the prophet Zechariah whom the Lord would use to encourage Zerubbabel.

In Chapter 1, we see the Horseman and the other red horses, a man among the myrtle trees (they patrol the earth for the Lord and bring Him tidings from all over). This is indicative of God's special care, purpose, and interest in His people. Aren't you glad of God's special care and concern for us? God is God, and God won't ever change. God is God, and He always will be God.

In Chapter 2, we see four horns and seven eyes on a stone. In this, we are assured of God's vengeance upon our enemies. This chapter speaks to the fact that the enemies are destroyed, and there is no longer any opposition to the building of God's house. So, *let God arise and let His enemies be scattered (Psalm 68:1-3, KJV).*

4

In Chapter 3, we see a man with a measuring line. This teaches us that Jerusalem will expand until it outgrows its wall, and God will be its best defense. This chapter tells us that Jerusalem will be a city without borders because of the power and might of God protecting it. God watches over the city because He is and always will be faithful. In this chapter, God rebukes the spirit of fear and intimidation from Joshua and places His anointing upon his life from the crown of his head to the sole of his feet. *How beautiful are the feet of those who bring good tidings of great things (Romans 10:15, KJV).* Because you have on the shoes of the gospel (Ephesians 6:15, KJV), you have beautiful feet. In Zechariah 3:2, we read how the Lord rebukes the devil, and we must know that *Jesus, our high priest, is yet making intercession for us (Hebrews 7:25, KJV). He is praying that we might be strengthened and that our faith will not fail when the enemy comes in like a flood and tries to sift us as wheat (Luke 22:32, Isaiah 59:19, KJV).*

In Chapter 3, we see Joshua, the high priest, clad in filthy garments, representing his sins and the people he was ministering to being cleansed and given charge of the temple. Yes, the temple of God is holy, and for us to minister effectively, *we must keep our body, which is the temple of the Holy Ghost, holy at all times (1 Corinthians 6:19, KJV).*

In Chapter 4, we see a seven-branched candlestick fed by two olive trees, teaching that the people of God will receive God's grace through their spiritual and temporal leaders, through whose efforts the nation's prosperity will be accomplished. *It will not be by might nor by power, but by my Spirit saith the Lord of Hosts (Zechariah 4:6, KJV).* We must understand that if we do not use our gifts to glorify God, we stand a good chance of losing them. All of our help comes from the Lord and not from human instrumentality. God will use others to do His work and us as well, but it is God who gives us the strength and power to do this work and not us. Even the work on our natural jobs and the things we do even in our own homes, this ability comes from God, and He and *He alone should get the glory (Isaiah 42:8, KJV)* for any and everything we can do.

In Chapter 5, we see a flying scroll (Zechariah 5:1-4), teaching that the land shall be purified from wickedness when the temple is built and God's law is introduced.

In Chapter 7, we see a woman (typifying the besetting sins of Israel) carried off to Babylon, which shows how God will forgive and carry their sins far away (Zechariah 5:5-11).

In Chapter 8, we see four war chariots going forth to protect God's people, teaching God's protective providence.

Now, after hearing from Zechariah, both Zerubbabel and Joshua were undoubtedly encouraged to do God's work, and now, we, after hearing from Zechariah, should be encouraged as well. This is another lesson on the Holy Ghost, and if you have not *spoken in tongues as the Spirit gives utterance (Acts 2:4, KJV),* you are missing out on one of the greatest spiritual blessings and experiences in your life. Do not just get to the edge of your blessing and then allow fear to keep you from getting the full effect of the Holy Ghost filling and baptism.

Zerubbabel had to know this: *For except the Lord keep the city, the watchmen wake but in vain and except the Lord build the house, the laborers labor but in vain (Psalm 127:1-2, KJV)*. It has to be done in God's time and in God's way.

David declared that *it is the Lord's doing, and it is marvelous in our eyes (Psalm 118:23, KJV). Let not the mighty man glory in his strength, neither let the wise man glory in his wisdom, but he that glories, let him glory in the Lord. The Lord will not give his glory to another (Jeremiah 9:23-24, KJV). Let us give Him or ascribe to Him all the glory due unto His name (Psalm 29:2, KJV).* Remember King Herod in the Book of Acts Chapter 10, who boasted in his own ability to get things done (James and Peter)? Then remember Nebuchadnezzar, who was cursed to eat grass like a wild animal (Daniel 4:24-35, KJV).

Let us run while the sun is shining. Let us run on in His name. *Work while it is the day, for when the night comes, no man can work (John 9:4, KJV).*

Daily Prayer

Dear God, as I begin this day, I release the reigns of my life into Your loving hands so that Your Holy Spirit will lead, guide, direct and use me to accomplish Your purposes in my life this day. Oh God, You are the Potter, and I am the clay, so dear Father, mold me and make me as I yield fully to You. Heavenly Father, thank You for the wonderful gift of time that You have given me. I shall use it wisely. In Jesus' name, I pray and give thanks, Amen.

CHAPTER 2

Do Not Become Confused In the Wilderness

Scripture Reference: Psalm 27, 34:1 KJV

My life is complex, but my praise is simple. Conditions in life can sometimes be complicated, disjointed, problematic, out of control, burdensome, stressful, uncertain, and, yes, even joyous. That is why it is so complex. We have both ups and downs in our lives at the same time. We are living and breathing, and that is good, but, at the same time, we are struggling to pay our bills, and on top of that, we are concerned about how to get well and overcome sickness and affliction. Then we are facing financial issues. Then we come to church, and the praise and worship leader tells us to forget about our problems and praise the Lord.

How can you praise Him when all of this stuff is going on in your life? Well, everything isn't going wrong, but everything isn't going well either. Yes, life is complicated with these ups and downs going on at the same time. But remember, although our lives are topsy-turvy, our praise is so simple because we will *bless the Lord at all times (Psalm 34:1, KJV)*. No matter what is going on, we should praise Him. Praise takes the complexities of life and simplifies them. Yes, praise takes away the worry and builds the faith of the child of God. Praise will cause the tears to dry up and the pain to go away. Praise reduces major complaints down to non-issues. If you just learn to glorify God in your situation, you will feel better, look better, smell better, and even better digest your food.

The complexities of life somewhat mirror what the Israelites had to face while in the wilderness. They were unable to simplify their complexities, which is why for 40 years, they had to be on punishment in the wilderness. Did you not know that *the wilderness and the complexities of life can be good for you (Psalm 119:71, KJV)*? Yes, it can be a place of growth, development, and increase. What happens when we do not entertain our wilderness experience properly? The wilderness is not a place to complain. The wilderness is not the place to become complacent about the things of God. The wilderness is not the time to be angry and upset with God, and it is not the place to start negative reflection and say things like, "I was better off before I came to the Lord."

Well, this is what happened to Israel in the wilderness. They allowed the demon of confusion to frustrate their calling, vision, purpose, and destiny. The demon of chaos is hard at work today in believers' lives, causing them to blame God instead of thanking God, causing them to doubt God rather than have faith in Him, causing many to backslide rather than persevere forward. Do not get lost in the wilderness.

Coronavirus, COVID-19, and the pandemic will not be a source of death for you, but I decree and declare that *you shall not die but live to declare the glory of the Lord in the land of the living (Psalm 118:17, KJV)*. Life is sometimes challenging but bless the Lord in spite of it. When sickness and afflictions attack your body, bless His name. Refuse to let anything, anybody, and any troubles, trials, tribulations frustrate your praise. Refuse to let your circumstances regulate your praise, but instead allow your praise to control your circumstances.

I can recall a time in my life when my money was funny, and my change was so strange. I was not sure as to how or where my family was going to get their next meal. This caused some frustration and worry for me as the head of my family. When I got to church that Sunday night, the enemy was getting the best of my mind and heart, and I was becoming doubtful, fearful, and discouraged. But in that service that night, I testified. Instead of a complaint and frustration coming out of my mouth, there arose praise out of my belly that turned my wilderness into an oasis, and this praise simplified my complicated situation. On that evening in church, I let my praise regulate my situation and not my situation control my praise. Yokes were destroyed, and I do not know how God turned my situation into a life of no struggles and into one of grace and supply. *He supplied my every need (Philippians 4:19, KJV),* and today, if I do not know anything else in this world, I know that praise is the gateway into the riches of heaven.

Do not become confused in the wilderness. When you are in the wilderness, give God high praise and begin to bless His name. Learn to reach deep down in your spirit, learn to lift Him even in your car, in your home, on your job, and yes, in the church too. We used to sing a song in the church that said, how did you feel when you came out of the wilderness leaning on the Lord? And the response would be, I felt like shouting, clapping, jumping, singing, shouting, etc. Today, allow your praise to turn your wilderness into a spiritual oasis. Allow God to turn your wilderness into tabled land. The song says, *"Lord lift me up, and let me stand, by faith on Heaven's tabled land. No higher plain than I have found, Lord, plant my feet on higher ground."* Another song says, *"My hope is built on nothing less than Jesus Christ and righteousness. I dare not trust the sweetest frame but wholly lean on Jesus' name. On Christ, the solid rock I stand, all other ground is sinking sand. All other ground is sinking sand."*

Your purpose is tied to your praise. And if the demon of confusion can keep you from your praise, he has at that time kept you from your purpose. It is essential to keep and maintain an attitude of gratitude and stay in a place of high praise. This is so that you will indeed fulfill your God-given purpose. The scripture says to *let the high praises of God be in our mouths as a two-edged sword in our hands (Psalm 149:6, KJV).* We can frustrate the enemy's plans through prayer *as we bind up the strong man and spoil all of his goods (Mark 3:27, KJV).* Let us wreak havoc on the kingdom of darkness and bind up the demon of confusion.

It is funny how the Apostle Paul had to defend his apostleship continually. He was a gospel giant, a gospel heavyweight, a miracle-working preacher, a bold and courageous leader, a sober and temperate saint. Despite his spiritual maturity and authority, his authenticity as a representative and ambassador for Christ was always under constant scrutiny and question. Therefore, we as saints must do what we know to do so that we may adequately represent Christ at all times (both in public and in private). Therefore, let us conclude that our praise is the antithesis of confusion, and as a result of our praise, we will fulfill our God-given purpose.

Daily Prayer

Dear Lord, You are all-wise and all-powerful, and You know what is best for me. Thank You for teaching me, O God, to walk in wisdom's way even in these critical and challenging times. I thank You that the weapon of praise has both stilled and even destroyed the enemy's plans. Thank You that, even in the wilderness, You have provided for newness and freshness by way of the high praises of God on my lips. Hallelujah, I give you praise. Amen.

CHAPTER 3

I Need A Refuge

Scripture Reference: Joshua 21:1-45 KJV

Joshua was a great and teachable leader. He knew how to listen and follow instructions from the Lord and those God had given to assist him. Nothing is known of his wife and children or even if he was married. But we know that in his epic speech to Israel, he said as for me and my house, we will serve the Lord. The implication is that he was married and had children, but it is only implied and not said. He was as good a follower as he was a leader, and this is a lesson that we can all emulate as it relates to relationships.

Joshua served the Lord wholeheartedly and was not one who would even think or dare to compromise. He was not given to bribery. He demonstrated great faith and excellent leadership abilities. He was fearless in his pursuit of righteousness and was guilty of possessing unquestioned loyalty and devotion to God and the things of God. He was not intimidated by others' strengths and giftings; he knew how to embrace and compliment others' ideas.

The Bible is right, and it tells us to *mark the perfect man and to behold the upright, for the end of that man is peace (Psalm 37:37-40, KJV)*. It does us no good to say they are good leaders and do not emulate their good traits. If that were the case, what good would it be to look at and compliment the goodness of others? Unless we follow their example, we are not better, but we are worse off for not following standards that the Lord places before us. We should just not read the Bible and not do what it says; we should read and heed it. The scripture says again that *the written things were written for our learning, that we, through patience and hope of the scriptures, might have hope (Romans 15:4, KJV)*. Life for us is much better when we do the book and not just read the book. Did not the word of God say, *be ye doers of the word and not hearers only (James 1:22, KJV)?* Again, the Bible says that we ought to *give the most earnest heed to the things that we have heard, lest at any time we should let them slip (Hebrews 2:1, KJV)*.

One of the saddest sights to see is a person who has let the word slip away from them. So, we read and study God's word with purpose, and that purpose is that after we have read it, we then apply what we have read to our everyday life. You may say, when you read it, you did not understand it. Go back, reread it, and then ask God for *wisdom to rightly divide it (2 Timothy 2:15, KJV)*. The Bible is a spiritual book, and one must be spiritual to understand and comprehend it.

Our testimony used to be that we are saved, sanctified, and filled with the Holy Ghost. Is that your testimony still on today? Are you yet saved, sanctified, and filled with the Holy Ghost? Jeremiah says *it is just like fire shut up in my bones (Jeremiah 20:9, KJV)*. Jesus said that *out of your belly shall flow rivers of living waters (St. John 7:37-38, KJV)*. *And ye shall receive power after that the Holy Ghost has come upon you, and you will be a witness unto Him (Acts 1:8, KJV)*. You have power in you today to lay hands on the sick. With your Holy Ghost power, you can cast the devil out. You can even lay hands on yourself. You can cast the devil out of your house, no matter how bad he wants to stay.

Satan, I cast you out of my house. Satan, I cast you out of my mind because my mind belongs to God. Satan, I cast you out of my place of employment. Satan, I cast you out of my church. You have the power. Now use it. You do not have to be scared or intimidated. You can lose all fear and bind satanic and demonic activities in your mind, your communities, your schools, and your neighborhood. Cast him out. Please do not ask him to leave; with your power, you *command and demand him to go in the name of Jesus (James 4:7, KJV).*

Yes, the world is hungry for the living bread. The world is thirsty for the water of life. Yes, they are hungry and thirsty for the word of God. We have it, and God mandates us to get this word out and share it with everyone we meet. Never let a witnessing opportunity pass by you.

In the beginning, God created Adam and Eve and not Adam and Steve. Neither did he create Sharon and Eve. Homosexuality is a sin in the eyes of God (Leviticus 20:13). He told the man and his wife to *be fruitful and multiply (Genesis 1:28, KJV),* and this can not happen when a marriage occurs between two people of the same sex. I still believe that marriage is only accepted in the eyes of God when it takes place between a man and a woman. It always has been, and it always will be.

The Bible also says that *marriage is honorable in all things, and the bed is undefiled in marriage (Hebrews 13:4, KJV).* The only place where the bed is honorable in the sight of God is the marriage bed. Suffice it to say that only married people should be doing the married thing. Why would you have to buy the cow when you can get the milk for free? What is going to happen when it comes to mama's baby and daddy's maybe? Young woman, you are more valuable than that. You are more beautiful than that. Young man, you are more valuable than that. No pressure should be placed on you, and you should not have to lower your morals and standards. He told me that I should do what he was asking me to do if I loved him. Well, you tell Jack that if he loved you, then he would not ask you to. We live in the age of the aggressive female and the bashful male. Do not lower your standards, and do not be bullied into doing things you know are outside God's will.

Yes, God is a keeper, and He will keep you if you want to be kept. None of us are perfect, and we all have made mistakes. Some of us act as if we have been perfect all of our lives, but some just never get caught if the truth be told. Abortion is a sin. I encourage you, single men, women, boys, and girls, to exercise total abstinence and allow God to work His perfect work in you. I do not advocate singles taking birth control; I advocate keeping your mind on Jesus and *letting Him keep you in perfect peace (Isaiah 26:3, KJV)*. I am just a voice crying in the wilderness, saying, prepare to meet your God because *He is soon to come (St. John 1:23, KJV)*.

My wife and I were blessed to be the proud parents of three beautiful daughters. While in our house, I am sure that they felt as if we were overly strict on them. Even if they wanted to go, there were certain places they would not ask because we did not support them going to parties, just hanging out without a purpose, going to clubs, worldly concerts. No, you would not play worldly music in my house, bring worldly music on tapes, etc. You were not going to stay out all night and come in any time of the day or night unless you were at a church service or a church concert; and if you were out, you were going to check in if you and a group were stopping by Denny's on the way back home. They went to the movies, school dances, talent shows, games, etc. They participated in whatever club at school and were allowed to participate in any extracurricular activity they wanted. They had my 100% support in all of their academic, music, and sports activities. Well, they may have some emotional scars (we all do) and may have missed out on some things that they may have wanted to be involved in, but today they are all okay, and they all love the Lord. We made plenty of mistakes as parents, of which I am sure, but God smiled on us in the midst of it all. I will not be guilty of knowingly allowing them to get into something I knew would not have been pleasing to God. I am not bragging because I have no bragging rights. I am still amazed at how things turned out. I am thankful that God did it for both my wife and me. All the glory, honor, and praises belong to God for the wonders He has done.

You need to get involved in a relationship. You need to go on dates and get to know your friend. I am not talking about Jim, Jack, Suzy, or Ann. I am talking about a heart-to-heart relationship with the Lord Jesus Christ. You need to get to know Him by spending time with Him, reading the scriptures, and asking the hard and challenging questions about growing in the Lord. Your life depends on it.

Joshua was a successful man because he stuck close to God and close to his leader, Moses. You can recover lost opportunities and begin fresh in God. God is a God of freshness and newness. He will make your life brand new. Tomorrow is not promised. *Now is the time to remember God (Ecclesiastes 12:1, KJV)*. Now is the time to be strengthened in your relationship with Him. Life can be full of surprises, but you can successfully face any challenge, past, present, or future, with the Lord on your side.

The cities of refuge were cities set aside for persons who committed a capital crime intentionally. If they just got to the city of refuge, then their lives would be spared. You have a city of refuge, a place to go for safety, comfort, and victory, and that is in Jesus. The Bible says *that the Lord's name is a strong tower, the righteous run into it, and there they are safe (Proverbs 18:10, KJV)*. Your situation is not too tough for God to handle. He specializes in mental and emotional ills. *Look to the hills from whence comes your help; your help comes from the Lord (Psalm 121:1, KJV)*. The Lord is willing to help us if we let Him in. He says I have seen your tears, and I have heard your cry. Drugs are not the answer. Your friends are not the answer. Suicide is not the answer. Alcohol and vaping are not the answer. But there is an answer to all of our problems and ills. Jesus has an outstretched arm for all of us today, and He is pleading for each of us to *come to His throne and find His help right there and right now (Hebrews 4:16, KJV)*. If you know that you need the Lord's help, come with your heart, mind, and spirit surrendered to God. Today can be the first day of the best days of your life. He is wanting and willing to help you now. Surrender your will to Him!

Daily Prayer

Oh Yahweh, Jehovah Nissi, I love, honor and adore You because of who You are. I ask, oh Lord God, that You would please forgive me for not trusting in You fully at all times. Thank You for another opportunity that You have given me to acknowledge You are my hiding place, shelter from the storm, and battle-ax in the time of battle. Yes, Lord, I will rest in You and not be anxious about conditions, circumstances, or situations. Thank You for teaching me to be still. Yes, it is in Your darling son Jesus' name I pray and give thanks. Amen.

CHAPTER 4

I Was Messed Up Until I Found Jesus

Scripture Reference: John 4 KJV

John Chapter 4 provides for us an exciting chapter in the life of Jesus. Though it is in its infant stages, we find that Jesus' ministry is now growing in popularity. His forerunner, John the Baptist, was no longer preaching because now his voice had been silenced by Herod and his wicked family. John the Baptist had preached concerning the coming of the Messiah before Jesus started His ministry. John told the people that He was coming and for them to get ready to receive Him upon His arrival. Yes, John preached in the wilderness of Judea and was baptizing those who were accepting his message of hope and change.

One day as John the Baptist was preaching and baptizing, Jesus showed up. At this point, John stops preaching and baptizing in the Jordan River and exclaims, "Behold the Lamb of God, who takes away the sin of the world." And who was this Lamb of God of whom John was speaking? Yes, it was Jesus himself. Why was John referring to Jesus as a lamb? Well, John spoke prophetically in that the prophet Isaiah had already mentioned over 700 years before, that *Jesus was led as a sheep to the slaughter, and as a lamb which was dumb, so he opened not his mouth (Isaiah 53:7, KJV).*

Now, when John the Baptist was standing there in the River Jordan, Jesus requests that John baptize Him. Upon such a request, John the Baptist was appalled and went into a long discussion about how Jesus should be baptizing him instead of him baptizing Jesus. Long story short, John finally baptizes Jesus. When this happened, the Bible says that the heavens opened and a light shines from heaven, the Holy Ghost lights upon Jesus in the form of a dove, and a voice thunders from heaven saying, *"This is my beloved Son, in whom I am well pleased" (Matthew 3:17, KJV).* Jesus was 30 years old at this time, and being of the age of 30, by Jewish law and tradition, He could now begin his ministry.

Jesus begins His ministry, and this is when John the Baptist's ministry begins to fade away. John said that *I must decrease, and He (Jesus) must increase (St. John 3:30, KJV).* John said *that I baptize you with water unto repentance, but He (Jesus) will baptize you with the Holy Ghost and with fire, and He (Jesus) would thoroughly purge His floor. He would gather the wheat into the granary, but the chaff He would burn with unquenchable fire (Matthew 3:11-12, KJV).*

Now the ministry of Jesus is soaring, and He is attracting a big following. And just like the religious leaders were upset with John the Baptist because of his following and message, these same Pharisees and Sadducees and Scribes are now displeased with the popularity and message of Jesus. They are seeking out ways to destroy Him. No wonder John the Baptist referred to these religious leaders as a *bunch of snakes, a generation of vipers*

(Matthew 3:7, KJV). Nothing has changed as it pertains to the human condition. Man still hates those who declare God's word and those who have made up in their minds to live for God. *The enemy wants to kill, steal, and destroy (St. John 10:10, KJV)* the church of God. Even Jesus says, *"Woe to you when all men speak well of you (Luke 6:26, KJV)."*

Because the ministry of Jesus was gaining popularity and it was in its beginning stages, Jesus returned to Galilee and went north. He did not want to reveal to the masses who He was this soon. He needed to get away from the crowd and retard His ministry's progress just a little until later on. The people loved Him. Now, Jesus' issues were not with those who did not claim to know God but with those who claimed that they were the true worshippers of God (the Pharisees and Sadducees). They hated the fact that the people had turned to the message of John the Baptist and Jesus instead of to them. This, for the Pharisees and Sadducees, translated into less income in their pockets and less influence in the society in which they lived. These religious leaders had amassed a lot of wealth, power, and authority, and now, they wanted nothing, not even Jesus, to interfere with that. Because of all the negativity associated with the ministry in Israel's Southern region, Jesus re-routes to the north.

Already opposition was rising against Jesus, especially from the Pharisees. They resented Jesus' popularity as well as His message, which challenged much of their teachings. Because Jesus was just beginning His ministry, it was not yet time to confront these teachers openly, so He left Jerusalem and traveled north toward Galilee.

But there is one problem. The scripture says that He must go through Samaria (St. John 4:4, KJV). What was the issue with going to Samaria, and why does the writer emphasize Jesus going through Samaria? Well, there is a little bit of history surrounding this story. After the northern kingdom, with its capital at Samaria, fell to the Assyrians, many Jews were deported to Assyria. Foreigners were brought in to settle the land and help keep the peace (2 Kings 17:24, KJV). The intermarriage between those foreigners and the remaining Jews resulted in a mixed-race, impure in the opinion of Jews who lived in the southern kingdom. Thus, the pure Jews hated this mixed-race called Samaritans because they felt that their fellow Jews who had intermarried had betrayed their people and nation. The Samaritans had set up an alternate center for worship on Mount Gerizim (St. John 4:20, KJV) to parallel the temple at Jerusalem, but it was destroyed 150 years earlier. The Jews did everything they could to avoid traveling through Samaria. But Jesus had no reason to live by such cultural restrictions. The route through Samaria was shorter, and that was the route He took.

It was not just because the route north was shorter through Samaria; there were other compelling reasons why Jesus chose to go through Samaria. Why did He go through Samaria? Some there needed the Word of God manifested in the flesh to appear to them and let them know that God had not forgotten them. God does have a blessing with your name written on it. These Samarian people were looked upon as dogs, outcasts, the scum of the earth, dregs of society, less than human, unworthy of salvation, and unworthy of God. Their relatives hated them and did not want to be associated with them. The Samaritans were looked down upon by their countrymen. But Jesus came to their town, not because it was a shorter distance to where He was headed, but because there was a need. There were people there who were hurting, depressed, out of touch, defeated, and unloved. Jesus knew that they needed to be touched and loved. He knew that they had waited for an answer long enough. Yes, this was going to be a great day of deliverance and change for this city. Well, this change started when Jesus met a woman of Samaria at the well.

Verses 5-6: Jesus strikes up a conversation with her by asking her for a drink of water (St. John 4:7, KJV). The woman's response is very cold and with a slight attitude. This woman had come to Jacob's well to draw water. Jacob's well was on the property originally owned by Jacob (Genesis 33:18, 19, KJV). It was not a spring-fed well but a well into which water seeped from rain and dew, collecting at the bottom. Wells were almost always located outside the city along the main road. Twice each day, morning and evening, women came to draw water. This woman came at noon, however, probably to avoid meeting people who knew of her reputation. Jesus gave this woman a special message about fresh and pure water that would quench her spiritual thirst forever.

Verses 7-9: This woman, a Samaritan, a member of the hated mixed race, was known to be living in sin and was in a public place. No respectable Jewish man would talk to a woman under such circumstances, but Jesus did. The gospel is for every person, regardless of race, social position, or past sins. We must be prepared to share this gospel at any time and in any place. Jesus crossed all barriers to share the gospel, and we who follow Him must do no less.

This woman was alone. This woman was experiencing a real-life need. She was thirsty. She was religious. She was racist and prejudiced. This woman was proud of her heritage and thought that she was better than the pure Jew. This woman was curious. This woman had a shameful past. This woman became convicted then convinced. This woman went to those with whom she was familiar and witnessed to them of the Messiah. The town became convicted and convinced. The town spent two days with Jesus.

Verse 10: What did Jesus mean by "living water"? In the Old Testament, many verses speak of thirsting after God as one thirst for water (Psalm 42:1; Isaiah 55:1; Jeremiah 2:13; Zechariah 13:1, KJV). God is called the fountain of life (Psalm 36:9, KHV) and the spring of living water (Jeremiah 17:13, KJV). In saying He would bring living water that could forever quench a person's thirst for God, Jesus was claiming to be the Messiah. Only the Messiah could give this gift that satisfies the soul's desire.

Verses 13-15: Many spiritual functions parallel physical functions. As our bodies hunger and thirst, so do our souls. But our souls need spiritual food and water. The woman confused the two kinds of water, perhaps because no one had ever talked with her about her spiritual hunger and thirst before. We would not think of depriving our bodies of food and water when they hunger or thirst. Why then should we deny our souls? The living Word, Jesus Christ, and the written Word, the Bible, can satisfy our hungry and thirsty souls.

Verse 15: The woman mistakenly believed that she would not have to return to the well each day if she received the water Jesus offered. She was interested in Jesus' message because she thought it could make her life more comfortable. But if that were always the case, people would accept Christ's message for the wrong reasons. Christ did not come to take away challenges but to change us internally and empower us to deal with problems from God's perspective. The woman did not immediately understand what Jesus was talking about. It takes time to accept something that changes the very foundations of your life. Jesus allowed the woman time to ask questions and put pieces together for herself. Sharing the gospel will not always have immediate results. When you ask people to let Jesus change their lives, give them time to weigh the matter.

Verses 16-20: When the woman discovered that Jesus knew all about her private life, she quickly changed the subject. Often people become uncomfortable when the conversation is too close to home, and they try to talk about something else. As we witness, we should gently guide the conversation back to Christ. His presence exposes sin and makes people squirm, but only Christ can forgive sins and give new life.

Verses 20-24: The woman brought up a prevalent theological issue—the correct place to worship. But her question was a smokescreen to keep Jesus away from her most profound need. Jesus directed the conversation to a much more critical point: the worship location is not nearly as important as the worshippers' attitude. *"God is Spirit" (St. John 4:24, KJV)* means He is not a physical being limited to one place. He is present everywhere, and He can be worshipped anywhere at any time. It is not where we worship that counts, but how we worship. Is your worship genuine and authentic? Do you have the Holy Spirit's help? How does the Holy Ghost help us worship? The Holy Ghost prays for us (Romans 8:26, KJV), teaches us the words of Christ (John 14:26,

KJV), and tells us we are loved (Romans 5:5, KJV). When Jesus said, "Salvation is from the Jews," He meant that only through the Jewish Messiah would the whole world find salvation. God had promised that *through the Jewish race, the entire earth would be blessed (Genesis 12:3, KJV).* The Old Testament prophets had called the Jews to be a light to the other nations of the world, bringing them to a knowledge of God, and they had predicted the Messiah's coming. The woman at the well may have known of these passages and expected the Messiah, but she did not realize that she was talking to Him.

Verse 34: The "food" about which Jesus was speaking was his spiritual nourishment. It includes more than Bible study, prayer, and attending church. Spiritual nourishment also comes from doing God's will and helping to bring his work of salvation to completion. We are nourished by what we take in and what we give out for God. In John 17:4, Jesus refers to completing God's work on earth.

Verse 35: Sometimes, Christians excuse themselves from witnessing by saying that their family or friends are not ready to believe. Jesus, however, makes it clear that around us, a continual harvest waits to be reaped. Do not let Jesus find you making excuses. Look around. You will find people ready to hear God's word.

I am glad that I met Jesus. I am so happy He changed my life. I am glad that He gave me a chance. I am glad He forgave me of all my sins. I am glad that He has given me a prosperous future. I am glad that He has put that living water down in my soul. I am glad that it is springing up into everlasting life. I may not be what I want to be but thank God I am not what I used to be. *I am a new creature in Christ (2 Corinthians 5:17, KJV).* Old things are passed away and behold, all things become new. Thank God for a change in my life, in my family, in my finances, in my mind, in my home, on my job, and even in the church. Oh, a great, great change has come over me, and I am no longer the same. Thank God I am free.

Daily Prayer

Thank you, Jesus, for being so patient with me and taking the time to work on my heart, soul, body, and mind. Oh, how I realize that I can do nothing without You and that I am nothing aside from thee. So again, Lord, search, purge, and cleanse me from all unrighteousness because I want to be fully and wholly thine. I confess that holiness shall be my watchword, and I vow to go into the hedges and highways and compel men, women, boys, and girls who are hopelessly and aimlessly lost to come to the Christ of God. Yes, I am committed to You. In the name of Jesus, I pray. Amen.

CHAPTER 5

Let Us All Go Back

Scripture Reference: Lamentations 5:21 KJV

Let's go back is a phrase that I have heard used in the church. It means there is something that was left behind, something that was not taught that used to be taught, something that is not being done that needs to be done, something that has died and needs to be resurrected, and something that used to be commonplace but is not so common anymore. This was not saying that we needed to repeat poverty, lack, and depression.

There is a press for old-fashioned holiness, where when we laid hands on the sick, they recovered. Yes, bring back those days—a time when we said what we meant and meant what we said. Bring back the time when we did not rush the service, but we just let the Lord have His way. Bring back those days when people received the Holy Ghost in Sunday School and got saved in choir rehearsal. Bring back the days of shut-ins. Please bring back the days when we called sin out, and there was no denial of it. Bring back the days when the church mothers trained ministers and young elders, not by just having a class, but by using the gift of discerning spirits and revelation knowledge. Bring back the days of the breakout of revival where our babies got saved and prophesied. Bring back the days when the young people cried out to God and received the

Holy Ghost's baptism. Bring back the days when the Holy Ghost filled our temple, our hearts, our minds, and our wills. Bring back the days when we did not let our tempers fly, the days when we did not get angry and did not walk around with attitudes. Bring back the days when we tried to walk and talk like Jesus. Bring back the days when we were humble, meek, mild, and full of compassion. Bring back the days when we *entered His gates with thanksgiving and into His courts with praise (Psalm 100:4, KJV)*. We need a revival in the land. Why do we need revival? We need a revival because there is a real famine and drought in the land. It is not a famine of bread and water because we have plenty of that. *There is a famine for hearing the word of God (Amos 8:11, KJV)*.

No, we do not preach like we used to preach. Preachers and missionaries do not labor in the presence of the Lord for a word from the Lord anymore. We are too busy for prayer meetings, too busy for Bible Study and Bible reading, too busy making money, and too busy looking at TV and listening to stuff we have no business looking and listening to.

What will it take for us to truly return to the old paths and seek the right way found in Jeremiah 6:16? Why ask for the old paths? It is because the new ways are delusional and destructive. The new methods are man's miserable substitution for the grand old "highway" of God, which only captivates the unsuspecting into Doubting Castle, the habitation of Giant Despair.

It is not optional for us to return to the old paths. It is a direct command from God. It is not a request. You can turn down an offer. The Lord does not require you to go to just any path but the old path. It is a clear path as well as the correct path.

During World War II, during the Battle of the Bulge, a group of German soldiers dressed in the allies' uniforms. These German soldiers used American military vehicles and went through the German countryside, changing the road signs. When the American troops came to the various crossroads, they were often fooled and led off in the wrong direction. The Germans' deception almost gave them victory in this very decisive battle from the Second World War.

Like those German soldiers caused confusion and death by changing a few signs, so many in our day are leading millions off into Hell because they are changing some of the faith's road signs. Yes, every word of God is right. It is time to repent of our sins, stop making excuses for being passive and calm about the King's business. Let us all take a serious look at our spiritual condition, take a serious self-evaluation and self-inventory, give ourselves an honest assessment and the resolve to go back to the old landmark, go back to the old-time way, fall on our faces, repent, and get back to the business of putting the Lord first in all that we say and do.

The old ways were when women looked like ladies, men looked like gentlemen, and children looked decent. The old ways were when people loved the truth and hated a lie. They would follow the Pastor and ignore the world. They came to get in and not to get out! The old ways were when cursing was wicked, drinking was evil, divorce was unbelievable, the flag was honored, America was beautiful, and God was welcomed. The old paths were when we read the Bible in public, prayed in school, and preached on the courthouse steps. The old paths were when laws were based on the Bible, homes read the Bible, and churches taught the Bible. The old paths were when preachers were more interested in new converts than new clothes and new cars. Churches wanted to reach every creature with the gospel more than new buildings and paved parking lots and prayed and wept over the lost in their community. The old paths were when God was worshipped. Christ was exalted, and the Holy Ghost was followed. The old paths were when the Bible was believed and not corrected, sinners got saved, converts were converted, and the gospel was preached and not shared.

Those were the days when we would go witnessing with tears, pray a lot, talk little on the phone, and spend more time with the Bible than the TV. We would weep about lost souls and enjoy going to church more than anything. We had testimony and song services. We would try to do something for God. We would say Amen to the truth and go to the altar to repent of sin. We would bring others to church, take Pastor home for Sunday dinner, and give tithes and offerings gladly. We would seek the will of God in everything and stand against sin anytime and anywhere. Those were the old paths.

Jeremiah was concerned about the present condition. As we look around the church world today, we see that we can use some old-time way preaching, teaching, singing, dancing, shouting, prophecy, and a visitation from the Lord. We must confess that we are in desperate need of a real-life altering touch from God. We should be tired of being touched and not being changed. We need an old-time revival where we speak in tongues as the Spirit gives utterance and prophesy under the Holy Ghost's real inspiration. In Acts 3:19, KJV, we read, *"Repent ye therefore, and be converted, that your sins may be blotted out when the times of refreshing shall come from the presence of the Lord."*

Lord, send a refreshing, send a fresh fire, fresh wind, fresh oil, and a fresh anointing. Psalm 63:1 says, *"O God, thou art my God; early will I seek thee: my soul thirsts for thee, my flesh longs for thee in a dry and thirsty land, where no water is"* (that is a result of falling prey to the new ways, which are not God's ways but are instead the ways of the works of the flesh). Psalm 91:1 says, *"He that dwells in the Most High's secret place (El Elyon) shall abide under the shadow of the Almighty (El Shaddai)."*

The way back to God is not mysterious, and nor is it without challenges and struggles. I challenge you to appeal to the Spirit of Christ that He will send times of refreshing from the presence of the Lord. Enter daily into early morning prayer time and reading of the word of God.

1. Find a scripture to meditate upon daily, even if it is the same one for a week.

2. Become a praiser and a worshipper and devote yourself to becoming a praying intercessor.

3. Place necessary and needed emphasis on studying the word of God for your individual personal growth in the Lord.

4. Walk in strict obedience to the revealed will of God and study to be quiet.

5. Consecrate often by fasting at least once or twice per week.

6. Sing and pray in the Spirit and seek to be filled with the Holy Ghost daily.

7. Identify and crucify the works of the flesh daily.

8. Attend services regularly and seek to reverence the spirit of Christ in the temple as you are standing on holy ground.

9. Intercede for your church and its leaders.

10. Strive to be a witness to someone daily by using social media if you have to.

11. Realize that you have been delivered from the three-fold curse of the Law (poverty, sickness, and spiritual death).

12. Seek to walk in liberty and victory daily.

13. Grow in the grace of God.

If you do these things, you will never fail (2 Peter 1:10, KJV) and develop and grow up in God. The Lord is on your side this day.

If you are not saved, if you are a backslider, if you are out of the ark of safety, give your life over to Jesus and experience new life, great peace, and overwhelming joy that all comes from knowing Jesus in a real way. God is concerned about you and your spiritual welfare. Let us all go back to the old paths and to the old-time way.

Daily Prayer

Thank You, dear Lord, for the blessed opportunity to petition You for a fresh anointing. I patiently wait in Your presence so that I can be filled the more with your Spirit. As I wait before You, I realize that I have fallen so short of Your glory by allowing the spirit of complacency and lackadaisicalness to retard my progress in spiritual matters. Father, I humbly ask that You renew my strength and restore my joy. Jesus, today I renew my vow to remain consecrated at my praying ground and to be available to and for Your service. In Jesus' name, I pray, Amen.

CHAPTER 6

Listen For The Trumpet Blast: It Is Time To Fight

Scripture Reference: Nehemiah 4:20 KJV

Nehemiah was a contemporary of Ezra. When the captives returned to Jerusalem after their 70 years of being in Babylonian captivity, Ezra led a group from Babylon back to the land of Israel; however, Nehemiah and others chose to remain in Babylon a bit longer. Ezra and the returning captives commenced working on the Temple; however, they merely laid the foundation and were chastised by God some decades later, scolding them for not completing the work. His warning to them was how could they feel so comfortable in their ceiled houses and just let the house of God deteriorate (Haggai 1:4, KJV). Those who had returned to Jerusalem were overwhelmed with all of the work that had to be done, so they just did nothing compared to what had to be done. It was at this time, the time when Nehemiah was enjoying a plush life in Babylon, working a prestigious job in the King's palace, that he received a visit from his brother Hananiah and others who had traveled from their hometown back to Babylon (a 600-mile trek) to see Nehemiah. They came with a message of concern and dismay. More than likely, most of those returning to Jerusalem had not even been born there but were born in captivity. They begin to rehearse to their brother Nehemiah how critical and challenging it was back in the homeland. Their fathers' land was overrun with wild beasts, and their Arabian enemies were continually taunting them and poking fun at them.

Did this concern Nehemiah at all? Yes, it did. This was not the news that he had wanted to hear. He wanted to hear of the progress of rebuilding and restoration. But instead, he heard the opposite of what he had wanted to hear. It is good to know that his knee-jerk reaction was not to go back to Jerusalem and whip those lazy Israelites into shape, nor was it to go back there and start a war with their enemies. His knee-jerk reaction was what ours should be. His first response was to go to God in prayer. What was his prayer? It was to have favor with his boss so that he could take a sabbatical to go to Jerusalem to correct some problems and possibly make a positive impact on his fellow countrymen. He needed favor with his boss, the King of Babylon or Persia, as it was called in his day because it was a matter of life and death when approaching King Artaxerxes (possible husband of Esther). God gave him favor, and he was able to make his request to the king. Pray about everything and take nothing for granted.

Not only was Nehemiah given favor, but the king also granted him his sabbatical. The king also ensured that he had border crossing documents, building material, and peace from all whose borders he may enter. Nehemiah got home to Jerusalem and was so devastated by what he saw. Again, his knee-jerk reaction was to consult God in prayer as to what his next move should be. Being led by God, he took a solo survey of the need for rebuilding. God is a wise God and knows how to direct His people. Why did he go alone to survey the city? It was because of dream killers, naysayers, wagging tongues, and gossipers. People have a way of discouraging you when they should be supporting you and pushing you forward. Don't listen to negative people when God has given you a job to do. Like Nike, just do it (John 2). After taking a careful and detailed look, he chose to make his number one priority be rebuilding the walls. Like the new Jerusalem will have 12 gates, the ancient Jerusalem had 12 gates to it. God gave Nehemiah a brilliant plan to reconstruct the walls of Jerusalem. It was so brilliant and simple that the enemies got upset and did everything within their power to stop the work until he began the work. This brilliant plan was to have each clan, group, or family who lived close to where one of the gates was responsible for building that section of the wall and gate. First of all, he commanded that they construct the 12 gates, and when the gates were completed, it was their job to connect the gates and to put the doors on the gates.

Their enemies were so upset that Nehemiah had taken an avid interest in the welfare of his brethren in Jerusalem, so much so they began to taunt, talk, stir up trouble, and tell lies on them. They reported false information back to the king and governors. They laughed and talked because they did not believe that this job would ever get started well, let alone completed. Nehemiah had a relationship with God and was not afraid to confront or ignore his enemies as the case would so dictate. The scriptures list the leaders of the enemy forces against them as Gershom, Sanballat, and Tobiah. They were their foes and troublemakers. They were thorns in their sides. But the people of God, who Nehemiah was leading, did not quit or give up.

When the enemy heard of their progress on the wall's rebuilding, they began to devise a plan to wage an unprovoked war against them. The venom of their hatred began to be more pronounced than ever. If you decide to give up and stop just because of some difficulty, guess what, you will never get anyplace. Keep it moving in the service of the Lord. I don't know about you, but I can do all things through Christ who strengthens me. There is a song that says that the darkest hour is just before the break of day. Nehemiah was near finishing this major building project when the enemy became more pronounced and furious against them. When the enemy was plotting to wage war, Nehemiah and his people began to pray. For the weapons of our warfare are not carnal, but they are mighty through God to the pulling down of strongholds. Even during their prayers and undaunting faith in God, some of the Israelites heard their enemies' negative words such as calling them pathetic, calling them, in other words, religious nuts, ignorant and stupid for trusting in their so-called God. Still, they were hurting words and sparked a spirit of discouragement among some of the people of God. Then they started saying stuff like – yeah, maybe they are right, and perhaps we need to quit. Our hands are tired, our strength is gone, and these stones are just becoming too much and too heavy for us to even think about trying to move them.

The plan is when life serves you a lemon, you need to make lemonade. In essence, this is what Nehemiah did. Since God had made known to them the plan of the enemy's surprise attack, Nehemiah now knew precisely how to ward off such an attack.

As Nehemiah was strategizing, the Jews who lived near the enemy came and told us again and again, "They will come from all directions and attack us!" He was wise enough by the Spirit of God to place armed guards behind the lowest parts of the wall in the exposed areas. He stationed people to stand guard by families, armed with swords, spears, and bows. As he continued to look over the situation, he called the nobles and the rest of the people together and told them to listen to me and not be afraid of the enemy. Remember the Lord, who is great and glorious, and fight for your brothers, sons, daughters, wives, and homes. Will you lay down and die or stand up and fight. Remember, it is worth fighting for.

When Sanballat, Gershom, and Tobiah heard that Nehemiah and the children of Israel knew their plans of a surprise attack, the enemy became very frustrated and lost their enthusiasm for moving forward with their plans of attack. Because the enemy became frustrated, confused, and baffled, the Israelites went back to work on the wall. But this time, when they returned to work on the wall, the Lord had given them a different mindset. No more was it just business and building as usual. This time when they returned to their work on the wall, it was with a mindset of being ready and prepared for war at a moment's notice just in case the enemy decided to do something stupid, like trying to attack them just because.

They were always prepared for war, even as they worked on the wall. So, only half of the men worked from then on while the other half stood guard with spears, shields, bows, and body armor. The leaders stationed themselves behind the people of Judah who were building the wall. Those who worked directly on the wall did it with one hand supporting their load and one hand holding a weapon. All of the builders had a sword (the word of God) belted to their side. The trumpeter stayed with the leader, Nehemiah, to sound the alarm. The King's business requires haste, and we do not have any time to waste. Because we are on business for the

King, each of us in our area of the vineyard often becomes so scattered, and as a result, we are more vulnerable to the enemy's attack.

You know how animals attack in the animal kingdom, be it a wolf, lion, tiger, or bear. These attackers will seek out from the herd those who are weakest, and when they are alone and away from protection, they will take them out and destroy them, eating them alive. This is the same strategy of the devil against the saints. So, to prevent this type of destruction over those scattered over this vast wall project, Nehemiah devised a plan to call the people together if necessary to go from building to fighting. He told them that I am the leader, watchman, and responsible for you all. I will keep an eye out for the enemy from all directions, and when I see him on the attack against us, I will have the trumpeter, who is always with me, to sound the alarm. This trumpet sound will alert all of us to go to the rallying point to launch our explosive attack on our enemy. But wait, he said, all we need to do is simply come together and pray because our God will fight for us. He will send forth his war-fighting angels. He will send legions of angels to war on our behalf. You shall hold your peace, and the Lord will fight for you. The trumpet sound was a call to war, prayer, praise, and worship. The trumpet call was a clarion call to unify with a common cause against a common enemy. It was a call to take on the enemy without fear, favor, or compromise. We need to listen to that sound. The sound that calls us to undignified praise and worship.

Those builders on that wall had to work with one hand and hold the sword with the other. They only came down off of the wall to wash their clothes. We serve a great big and powerful God, and therefore, we do not need to fear what our enemies will do to us. David said, *"I will bless the Lord at all times, and His praises shall continually be in my mouth." (Psalm 34:1, KJV)*

Tobiah, Sanballat, and Gershom were working in the spirit of witchcraft, which is manipulation by intimidation for domination, and we know that rebellion is as the sin of witchcraft. We must understand that we can do all things through Christ who strengthens us because there is no failure in God. There is nothing beyond the wisdom of God because while you are trying to figure it out, He has already worked it out. Do not walk in fear of the enemy. God has already taken care of it. All He needs for you to do is *stand still and see the salvation of the Lord (Exodus 14:13, KJV)*. Get out of God's way and let God be God. He holds the world in the palm of His hands. *He made the stars, and He calls each of them by name (Psalm 147:4, KJV)*.

The enemy tried to trick Nehemiah away from the job God had given him to do. They did not take Nehemiah seriously. They tried laughing and taunting. They resorted to verbal threats and tried to push him around. They tried fake diplomacy. They sent a formal letter of invitation to meet at a designated place at a prearranged time. Again, Nehemiah's knee-jerk reaction was not one of falling for the trick of those who were harboring evil intentions. He was consulting the Lord in prayer. Nehemiah knew how to put a prayer on it, and he knew how to get a prayer through. So that is what he did. When those lying enemies came to him for his response, his answer was, why should the work cease (Nehemiah 6:3, KJV).

It was a tough job, but because they worked together, they were able to complete the job in record time. Instead of being intimidated by the enemy, we should not only have a knee-jerk reaction of prayer, but we should also have a knee-jerk reaction of praise. Both prayer and praise are defensive weapons against the enemy. We are in a war, and it is a serious battle in which we are engaging. Put your war clothes on and get ready to put a prayer on it and get ready to put a praise on it. Stop quitting, stop getting discouraged and learn how to pray and praise your way out of your situation.

Everybody cannot hear the trumpet. You need to have a spiritual ear to hear this sound. It may just come in the middle of the night (Praise is that sound).

The Bible declares that *praise is comely for the upright (Psalm 33:1, KJV)*. In other words, it is as common for saints to praise God as it is for one to breathe. The scripture tells us to *let everything that has breath praise the Lord (Psalm 150:1, KJV)*. There is something about praise that pleases God. There is a secret that the enemy likes to keep hidden from the people of God, and that is that when the praises go up, the blessings and the blesser come down. Praise not only pleases God, but it brings with it such a spiritual dynamic that results in victory for the one who is praising God. You not only have a right to praise God, but you have a spiritual responsibility to do so as well. This spiritual dynamic is beyond human explanation and human reasoning. I say this because God uses praise as medicine for the body, soul, and spirit. In and through praise and worship, our spiritual eyes are open, and our situations receive the miracle touch of God. If you can praise Him in times of trouble and distress, then you are surely next in line for a miracle.

It is in this that we see and understand that *all things work together for good for those who love God (Romans 8:28, KJV)*. In this time, we know that what the devil meant for evil, God has already turned it around and worked it for our good. It is in this spiritual moment that we experience our greatest power and our greatest anointing. This is when we can tell the devil to put a sock in it. This is when we can *resist the devil, and he will flee from us (James 4:7, KJV)*. This is our heritage and our rightful place in God at all times. The devil should not be beating up on you; you should be beating up on him. He is a defeated foe. *Let God arise and His enemies be scattered (Psalm 68:1-3, KJV)*.

We must understand that when we praise God, God at that time may not mitigate or change our circumstances. Still, in the moments of praise, God changes us from fear to faith, from weakness to strength, from sadness to joy, from sickness to health, from broke to rich, from depression to unspeakable joy, from poverty and lack to riches untold. In the moments of praise and worship, our understanding is enhanced, and our perspective has become spiritual instead of natural. The miracle of praise will indeed result in a closer relationship with God and a deeper understanding of our fellow man. If you praise God the more, then your mind and heart will be at rest and peace. Praise and worship cannot abide with confusion and complaining. They cannot and will not abide in the same house. That is why it is so important to have an attitude of gratitude at all times. Anger and praise cannot live in the same place.

In praise, revelation knowledge is heightened, and spiritual understanding increases. Now you should see and understand why the enemy wants to keep your life and mind away from praise.

Praise and worship are potent weapons that the Lord has given to the saints to express the purpose of living a worry-free and victorious life in Christ Jesus. I am saying that keeping your mind stayed on Jesus is the way to have, maintain and continually experience perfect peace (Isaiah 26:3, KJV).

What are you expecting to receive from the Lord? What are you waiting for and on? Why does the praise and worship team have to ask you to praise the Lord when the Bible tells us that praise is a common thing for the people of God? That is why David instructs us to *enter into His gates with thanksgiving and into His courts with praise (Psalm 100:4, KJV)*. In other words, enter in praising the Lord. Give God your best praise at all times. Do not be ashamed to let God have His way in your life. Do not fuss or argue in your mind about it. Just let God do what He wants to do in you. It is and can be just a simple matter of just doing what the Bible has told you to do in the area of praise. We are instructed to *clap our hands (Psalm 47:1, KJV)*. We are instructed to *praise God in the dance (Psalm 149:3, KJV)*. We are to *shout unto God with our voices (Psalm 47:1, KJV)*. We are to *sing songs unto Him (Psalm 105:2, KJV)*. We are to *lift our hands (Psalm 134:2, KJV)*. We are to *teach our sons and daughters to praise God (Deuteronomy 11:19, KJV)*.

Always keep the Lord on your mind. Let nothing or no one frustrate your praise. When situations and people seem to be hindering your praise, you must at that moment begin to become radical and undignified in your praise. And when they try to stop you or make fun of you, you need to dig down even deeper and come on out with more undignified praise. This will take you to levels in the spirit that you never thought possible. When you praise Him, you cause His favor to rest on you. When you praise Him, you are living and walking in big.

God is performing a spiritual operation on us all even now. He is changing us from the inside out and not necessarily from the outside in. What are you going to do with your problems? Your life will change dramatically and supernaturally when you tap into the secret of praise and worship.

Our God inhabits praise (Psalm 22:3), KJV). For the chains that seem to bind you serve only to remind you that they fall powerless behind you when you praise Him.

Daily Prayer

Father, thank You for the weapon of praise. Thank You for the sound that alerts me to the call for battle, the sound that unifies the saints so that miracles, signs, and wonders are on display for Your glory. Thank You, Father, that I am never defeated but always victorious because of the sound anointed by heaven. Father, I bless Your holy and highly exalted name. Amen!!!!

CHAPTER 7

Praise Your Way Through

Scripture Reference: Joshua 17-22 KJV

Joshua spoke prophetically (you can and will conquer giants, iron chariots, and all) and directly to the tribe of Joseph's complaint's fears (giants and iron chariots). One major mistake the Children of Israel made was that instead of utterly destroying some of the Canaanites, they allowed them to live as slaves and as people from whom they collected taxes or tributes. This was in direct contradiction to the Lord's original order and instructions.

In Joshua 18, the Tabernacle is set up in Shiloh. Seven tribes have not received their inheritance. Three men from each tribe are tasked to go out and describe and divide the land. This entailed creating a map of it in a book and bringing the notes back to Joshua. Joshua would then cast lots (pull names out of a hat or pull straws) to see which tribe gets what. Then the tribes were to go out and possess the land the best they could because it had already been conquered. All they had to do now was possess it.

In Joshua 19:47-48, the tribe of Dan's assigned territory was too little, so they went and took the territory and then renamed it Dan. Yes, once you take possession of a thing, you have the privilege of changing its name. You can do with it whatsoever you want because it is yours.

We must be careful not to do more than one thing at a time, and we must *do things decently and in order not to create confusion (1 Corinthians 14:33, 40, KJV)*. One thing at a time. After the land had been conquered, Joshua divided their portion of land out to the various tribes. The tribe of Levi, the priestly tribe, had no land for their inheritance. Through Joshua, the Lord said that the priest's office was to be their inheritance instead of land or real estate. Being a priest far outweighed that of being just a landowner. It was the responsibility of the landowners to ensure that the priests were taken care of. The next thing was to establish cities of refuge. The city of refuge was a place of safety. It was a place of freedom and peace. It was a place a person could breathe and find solace and comfort. Peace, security, ease, comfort, and rest should have been something they could experience in their cities or hometowns.

Why were they leaving the comforts of home to find safety in a place that was not their hometown? It was because if a person committed a capital offense, murder by accident, they were allowed by law to go to another place to be free from bounty hunters and angry members of the murdered victim's family. Where can we go when the storms of life are raging? Where can we go when the winds of sorrow blow? Where can we go in times of tribulations? Where can we go when there is no place else we can turn? Is there a refuge for the saints? Yes, you already know, we go to the *rock of our salvation (Psalm 89:26, KJV); we go to the stone that the builders rejected (Psalm 118:22-23, KJV)*. You can run and tell Jesus. He will not turn you away. He will surely heal you. He will set free and deliver in a time of stress. He will give you peace of mind and cause the storm clouds to roll away.

There are times in our lives when people will not understand the depth of the pain that we sometimes, as humans, have to endure. There are situations that the Lord will have us face without the assistance of anyone else. Tests and trials are not allowed by God in our lives to cause us harm or hurt. He will enable them to make us stronger so that we can, in turn, go higher in Him and, as a result, be able to help others who may be in affliction. We do not hang our heads down in the tough times, but instead, we do as the scripture commands us – we glory in tribulations (Romans 5:3, KJV).

What does it mean to glory in tribulation? It means we pray our way through. It means that we dance our way through. It means that we press our way through when we cannot sing or shout our way through. We go through in the name of Jesus. Yes, *He is our refuge and our hiding place (Psalm 32:7, KJV)*. Sometimes we are so guilty of making it hard for people to enter into the city of refuge. What we do is lock the gates to the city and turn out the lights. We do not let them forget their past, and we refuse to forgive them for their past mistakes. Believe it or not, people do at times genuinely change, and all they need is a little breathing room from us to move freely throughout the city without proving that they are saved and changed. If you harbor unforgiveness and resentment, let it go and let the people that you resent go too. Never is the failure in God; it is always in us. Forgive, forget and move on.

The next thing was to hear a complaint from the priestly tribe, the tribe of Levi. Now, they make their way to Shiloh, the place where the Tabernacle is located. The Tabernacle was always centrally located to give equal distance access to the place of corporate worship. Levi's tribe requested that they be given portions of land in each of the tribes' locations for herding and feeding their cattle. This request was a no-brainer, and Joshua immediately granted it.

We must seek to be noble, friendly, trustworthy, civil, sensible, kind, and cordial to all men. When you make your request known, you should live in great expectancy of your request. You must consecrate your requests before you make them. Everything that you are asking God for may not always be what you should be asking. When we do not know what or how to pray, *the Holy Ghost will intercede for us on our behalf (Romans 8:26-27, KJV)*. The Holy Ghost knows what to tell God and knows what we need to pray for and ask. You must know God knows when, where, and how to grant your requests. One of the main things we need when making a request is patience. Because it is in your patience that you possess your soul. We must consecrate our requests before we ask. Philippians 4:6 says, *"Be careful or anxious for nothing, but by prayer and supplication, with thanksgiving, let your requests be made known unto God."* Then after you ask, you need to put a praise on it, not a whine or pity party on it, but put a praise on it.

After dealing with the Levites' request, Joshua talked to three of the most faithful and patient tribes in all Israel, the tribes of Reuben, Gad, and the half-tribe of Manasseh. These are referred to as selfless and giving tribes. They chose and agreed to assist with all of the other tribes struggling to conquer their enemies and fully possess their portions of the land. Now the land did not belong to Rueben, Gad, or Manasseh; however, they fought just as hard as those to whom the land belonged.

Sometimes when you are in the midst of a struggle, the best God-designed therapy is that you forget about yourself and begin to help and assist someone else who may be in need. Joshua encouraged them and commended them for their untiring and selfless service to the community of believers and saints. Sometimes, you may even have to encourage yourself in the Lord (1 Samuel 30:6, KJV). You must know that you are doing the right thing and that God is pleased with your life. Curveballs are a fact of life, and our God has given us the wherewithal to deal with every circumstance that comes our way. Joshua encouraged them and then told them to go home and have a big celebration of victory. Relax, celebrate, rejoice, and receive blessings from the Lord. Yes, you fought a good fight (2 Timothy 4:7-8, KJV). *Rejoice (Philippians 4:4, KJV)*. You conquered all of your fears. You survived the battle and the trials.

Now have a praise party. You went into the fire and came out without the smell of smoke on you (Daniel 3:26-27, KJV). Now sing about that. What the devil meant for evil, the Lord truly worked it out for your good. And you can tell the devil that it isn't over until He (God) says it's over and I do not look like what I have been through.

The three tribes went home. They had to go to the other side of Jordan because the Jordan River separated them from the other tribes. They built an altar to commemorate the faithfulness of God for allowing them to get back home. When the other ten tribes got word about them building this altar, they got so upset until they wanted to go to war with them because they thought they were turning away from Jehovah and trying to start their own church. It's okay to have a zeal for God (Romans 10:2, KJV), but your enthusiasm must be tempered with wisdom, knowledge, and common sense, and definitely with consecration and prayer. Stay away from hasty fleshly decisions. They will get you in trouble every time.

Now, these ten tribes got all geared up and went to face these three tribes. They confronted them with a charge of treason against God. Their charge was soon proven to be untrue, and the three tribes convinced them that they were trying to have some church and thank God for where they were located, rather than have to travel hundreds of miles just to go to church in Shiloh. You may have to stop a few minutes and convince the haters of your true purpose, but please do not let the haters steal your joy. Instead of pouting about their complainers, the three tribes went back to having church. Let nothing or no one frustrate your praise. Do not let pride, anger, arrogance, or frustrated money hinder your praise. Do not let your friends stop your praise.

Daily Prayer

Oh, wonderful Savior, I praise and magnify Your name. I find myself in every condition, situation, or circumstance, giving You thanks. Yes, You have truly given me more than what I deserve. Oh, Father, I surrender to Your will, You are in charge, You are in control—Yes Lord, have Your way in my life. So Lord, on this day and in this hour, I give thanks for Your faithfulness. In the matchless name of Jesus, I pray, Amen.

CHAPTER 8

Christ, the Savior and the Baptizer in the Holy Ghost

Scripture Reference: Romans 3:23 KJV

The book of Romans brings us such powerful messages. The powerful messages are shining through so brightly—the message of faith, the power of the Gospel, the condition of lost humanity without God, lost in sin—under the power of the enemy—Satan himself. Jews and Gentiles alike, black, white, brown, and any other persons or individuals, are all lost—*for all have sinned and come short of the Glory of God (Romans 3:23, KJV)*. But as a powerful jet stream and bombshell comes into the world, is one who can save and deliver, to free man from his demons and bondages, from his inevitable death-sad condition of hopelessness, just like you and I were before we knew the Lord.

Isaiah 53 says that we all, like sheep, have gone astray, sheep without a shepherd, lost and wandering. Your days of wandering and searching are over because Jesus came into the world. There was no welcome committee to greet the King of Kings, no red carpet to honor Him, no horses, and chariots of fire, but into a humble beginning, He entered. From the days of His birth, Satan was trying to destroy the Son of Promise. It started with His birth in a barn or maybe even with Joseph, who probably wanted to abort Him, but He came anyhow. He grew up in the gangster town of Nazareth, the Nazareth projects, the ghetto town of Nazareth. He came to set the captive free, to make life better for you and me. He came that our faith could go on and increase.

According to the scriptures, righteousness (right living and right standing with God) results from exercising faith in God. Faith is believing with personal trust and confident reliance on Jesus Christ and is something that each saint possesses. But everyone, saints and sinners alike, has faith in someone or something. It is crucial to build good Christian faith on solid principles, even and expressly, God's word.

In Romans 10:14-17, we read, *how then shall they call on Him in whom they have not believed? And how shall they believe in Him of whom they have not heard? And how shall they hear without a preacher? And how shall they preach except they are sent? As it is written, how beautiful are the feet of them that preach the gospel of peace and bring glad tidings of good things!* But they have not all obeyed the gospel. Isaiah the prophet said, *"Lord who has believed our report, and to whom is the arm of the Lord revealed? So, then faith cometh by hearing and hearing by the word of God."*

We need faith to allow God the right of way. The problem is that we have faith, but we do not have the now faith. We stop at the then faith, but by faith, *God called those things that are not as though they were (Romans 4:17, KJV).* You need to know beyond the shadow of a doubt that you are saved. If you are saved, you are a candidate for the baptism in the Holy Ghost. But if you are not thoroughly convinced that you are saved, you will not be effective in your verbal and silent witnesses. There is a need for those baptized in the Holy Ghost to be refilled with the Holy Ghost regularly.

Have you received the Holy Ghost like the Bible said since you believed (Acts 19:2)? The physical evidence of the Holy Ghost baptism and filling is found in Acts 2:4. You will speak in a new tongue unbeknownst to yourself when you are filled and baptized in the Holy Ghost. Speak and pray in your heavenly language. When we speak and pray in tongues or our heavenly language, we build ourselves, and our faith increases due to this Holy Ghost intensified dialogue (Jude 1:20, KJV). Be convinced and sure that you are saved because you will continuously be defeated if you are not.

We strengthen our faith through prayer, for if we believe, we shall indeed receive. Mark 9:22-26 says, *and Jesus answering saith unto them, Have faith in God. For verily I say unto you, That whosoever shall say unto this mountain, Be thou removed, and be thou cast into the sea; and shall not doubt in his heart but shall believe that those things which he saith shall come to pass; he shall have whatsoever he saith. Therefore I say unto you, What things soever ye desire when ye pray, believe that ye receive them, and ye shall have them. And when ye stand praying, forgive if ye have ought against any: that your Father also which is in heaven may forgive you your trespasses. But if ye do not forgive, neither will your Father which is in heaven forgive your trespasses.*

Your faith is strengthened through the word of God. Psalm 119:105 says *thy word is a lamp unto my feet and a light unto my pathway.* What can your faith do for you? Matthew 7:7-11 says to *ask, and it will be given to you; seek, and you will find; knock, and it will be opened to you. For everyone who asks receives and the one who seeks finds, and to the one who knocks, it will be opened. Or which one of you, if his son asks him for bread, will give him a stone? Or if he asks for a fish, will give him a serpent? If you then, who are evil, know how to give good gifts to your children, how much more will your Father who is in heaven give good things to those who ask Him.*

Mark 10:52 says, and Jesus said to him, *"Go your way; your faith has made you well. And immediately, he recovered his sight and followed him on the way."*

Acts 16:31 says, *"Believe on the Lord Jesus Christ, and thou shalt be saved, and thou house."*

Mark 16:17-18 says, *"And these signs will accompany those who believe: in my name, they will cast out demons; they will speak in new tongues; they will pick up serpents with their hands; and if they drink any deadly poison, it will not hurt them; they will lay their hands on the sick, and they will recover."*

Many of us need to have our faith in God strengthened even as we seek and anticipate a refilling in the Holy Ghost. Fill us again, God; we want to be an effective witness and experience victorious Christian living. We need to be made whole and complete in Him. Some appear to be strong, but in actuality, they are as weak as water, not stronger than a gnat when it comes down to suffering for righteousness sake (Matthew 5:10, KJV). We complain too much. Again, we must not trust in our strength to deliver ourselves. Only God can deliver; only God can do it. And He does it through the preaching of the Gospel, the teaching of the word of God, and the receiving thereof. When we receive the word of God into our spirits, this will give us a way into the spiritual things of God. Instead of spending time on TV and Facebook and idle workings, we need to use our time to stay in the face of God. This will cause spiritual increase and power with God.

We have peace with God and divine access into this grace (Romans 5:1, KJV). Stay strong and feed the Holy Ghost with fasting and prayer.

Stay in the upper room until Shiloh comes. Remain in place until the Holy Ghost power takes over.

Daily Prayer

Oh God, in times like these, I am more aware now than ever that I need an outpouring of Your Spirit upon me. Please send a refreshing, refill me with the Holy Ghost and empower me to go forth and bring in the sheaves, the great harvest of souls. Thank You for the refrain in my soul that constantly rings out, "Spirit of the living God, fall fresh on me" and "Let the power of the Holy Ghost fall on me." Thank you, God, that my soul will be satisfied and my heart will be renewed. Thank you. In Jesus' name, Amen.

CHAPTER 9

Take It By Force

Scripture Reference: Daniel 11:3; Matthew 11:12 KJV

For many of us, the word 'force' is a very unkind and demeaning type of word. It is a word that we have heard a lot of in the media. The term 'force' is associated with the word 'rape.' It has a highly negative connotation when discussing the police. Excessive force, unnecessary force, and extreme force are terms used to describe the police relationship with the communities they are hired to serve and protect. The word force has a negative meaning when discussed in conjunction with child abuse, sweat factories, human trafficking, drug use, abuse, and distribution. Force is a way of life for gangs, cartels, mafia, child porn rings, and money laundering. Where is all of the money? A lot of it is with the wicked, but the wealth of the wicked is stored up for the righteous.

Regardless of the pandemic, the will of God for His people is to be blessed despite the pandemic and even amid the pandemic. The number 20 in the Bible symbolizes the cycles of completeness. It is not so widely used, but it is often connected to a perfect waiting period, labor, or suffering compared to a trial and rewarded. Jacob waited 20 years to get his wives and property and be released from his father-in-law, Laban. Solomon built a house for himself and God for 20 years until he obtained a place to live. Jabin, the Canaan king, oppressed Israel's people for 20 years until Deborah and Barak managed to release people from the trouble. God told Abraham that if he finds at least 20 righteous people in Sodom and Gomorrah, He will not ruin them.

The number 20 is associated with a trial, a waiting period, and if it is completed, the reward is generous and full of God's love. In the other case, if not completed successfully, the punishment is then just and right.

Expect a miracle every day; God will make a way out of no way. In pain, understand that *weeping may endure for a night, but joy comes in the morning (Psalm 30:5, KJV)*. In the book of Daniel, we read concerning how the enemy's attack will be so great against the saints of God until he will wear the saints out; however, the people who know their God will do exploits (Daniel 7:25, 11:32, KJV).

We shall know who He is when we see Him without anyone telling us who He is (1 John 3:2, KJV). When the disciples first started following Jesus and saw Him heal the sick, turn water into wine, feed 5,000 with two fish and five barley loaves, and heal the blind, they thought they knew Him. Still, when He instructed them to board the ship and go to the other side of the lake Gennesaret or the sea of Galilee, they saw a side of Jesus that they had never seen before. The sea got so boisterous, and the waves became so contrary. The disciples became fearful and anxious, but they cried out until they woke the master, who was taking a nap on board the ship. When He got up and took control of nature by the words of His mouth, they said one to another, we thought we knew Him, *but what manner of man is this that even the wind and the waves obey*

Him (Matthew 8:27, KJV). Neither Muhammad nor Buddha could do this, and the miracles that Jesus performed are not recorded as being performed by them. Get to know Him. *The people who know their God shall be strong and do exploits (Daniel 11:32)*. Know Him as:

- Jehovah Jireh

- Jehovah Nissi

- Jehovah Rohi

- Jehovah Mkaddesh

- Jehovah Rophe

- Jehovah Sabaoth

- Jehovah Shalom

- Jehovah Shammah

- Jehovah Tsidkenu

- El Elyon

- El Shaddai

Many are the afflictions of the righteous, but the Lord delivers him out of them all (Psalm 34:19, KJV). Take it by force (Matthew 11:12). Close to the Garden of Gethsemane on the Mount of Olives, where Jesus said farewell to His beloved disciples, they asked Him a question, *"Lord, will thou at this time restore the*

Kingdom to Israel?" His response to them was, it is not for you to know the power that the Father has put in His own hands, *but you shall receive power after that the Holy Ghost has come upon you (Acts 6-8, KJV).* If you have the Holy Ghost, then you have Dunamis power. Explosive self-re-producing power is what you have. It will never run out. It does not matter if there is an oil glut or an oil drought; the Holy Ghost power will remain the same. You can take it by force because the force is within you. As the prophet told David, *you shall pursue, and without fail, you shall recover all (1 Samuel 30:3, KJV).*

We must admit that we are living in a crazy mixed up and confused world. People are bailing out on God and giving up on life. We can see how mean, hateful, uncaring, bruised, hurt, discouraged, hopeless, and helpless they are. The abuse of the mind by the enemy of the soul has caused people to be dropouts and sinister in their demeanor in many cases. God is only one prayer away. You are only one prayer away from your breakthrough.

There is a force that God has given to the church, and this force has been made available to every believer. This force has been known to set the captive free. It has been known to make a crazy man sane. It has been known to mend relationships that had at one time been destroyed. This force has caused even the most powerful nations to crumble and the richest men to become paupers. This force has converted nations, cleaned the dirtiest hearts, and made them as white as snow. This force has been known to make the drunk person sober. Foundational to every great move of God is what is called spiritual preparation. Did you not know that you are a child of the King? And as a child of the King, you are allowed and given royal rights and privileges. Use your royal force that has been granted to you by special powers and privilege to your spiritual advantage. Resist the devil, and he will flee from you. The force is not only with you, but the force is within you right now. If you believe that the God force is in you, lay hands on yourself and say be healed, delivered, and set free!!!

Many times, being spiritual will require you to talk to yourself. Many times, as a saint of God, you will be required to pray for yourself. This force brings with it so many spiritual blessings and victories. Power, peace, wisdom, freedom, and growth are some of the victories that we receive from this force that God has given to us.

The Apostle Paul has encouraged many of us. He said to the church of Ephesus, *"Finally, my brethren, be strong in the Lord and the power of his might" (Ephesians 6:10).* He says to the church of God *to put on the whole armor of God so that we will be able to stand. The weapons of our warfare are not carnal but spiritual. They are mighty through God to the pulling down of strongholds. For we wrestle not against flesh and blood, but powers, rulers of darkness, against spiritual wickedness in high places. Wherefore take unto you the whole armor of God. Take the helmet of salvation. You will need the breastplate of righteousness, the girdle or belt of truth, the shield of faith, feet shod with the preparation of the gospel of peace, and the sword of the spirit, which is the Word of God (Ephesians 6:11-17, KJV).* Fight the good fight of faith just like Jesus did. The scripture tells us that death could not hold Him down (1 Corinthians 15:20-22, KJV).

1 Corinthians 2:7-10 says, *"No, we declare God's wisdom, a mystery that has been hidden and that God destined for our glory before time began. None of the rulers of this age understood it, for*

if they had, they would not have crucified the Lord of glory. However, as it is written: What no eye has seen, what no ear has heard, and what no human mind has conceived the things God has prepared for those who love Him—these are the things God has revealed to us by His Spirit."

For this reason, the son of God was made manifest, that He might destroy the works of the devil (1 John 3:8, KJV). Death said to the grave, "Grave, if you hold Him, then I will sting Him." It is impressive how ignorant the enemy is in certain high and lofty spiritual matters. There are things that we know that he does not know. Jesus is the God-Man. He is 100 percent God and 100 percent man at the same time.

As the power of God would have it, the contract between death and the grave was made null and void by the resurrection of Christ from the dead, and He rose with all power in His hands.

Daily Prayer

Thank You, Lord, that I am blessed in the city and blessed in the fields. I am blessed going out and coming in. I confess that I can do all things through Christ, who strengthens me. I believe that no weapon formed against me can prosper because greater is He who is in me than he that is in the world. Father, I walk by faith and not by sight and call those things that be not as though they were. My confession is my possession. In Jesus' name, I pray, Amen.

CHAPTER 10

Remember What Jesus Said About Prayer

Scripture Reference: Luke 18:1-8 KJV

God said in Leviticus 11:44 to *be ye holy for I am holy,* and you cannot live holy without the Holy Ghost. We need Him in our lives, business, and even our jobs. Jesus commanded His disciples to go to Jerusalem and to tarry for the Holy Ghost. Even after His resurrection, He commanded His followers to go to Jerusalem and tarry or wait for the Holy Ghost.

Why is it necessary to be filled to overflowing with the Spirit of God? To be Spirit-filled is to be spirit controlled, animated, and talked to by the Holy Ghost. The post resurrected Christ lived and walked on this earth for 40 days after His resurrection. During these 40 days, He continued to break bread and fellowship with His disciples. At this time, He had a glorified body, which had been resurrected from the dead, which was now able to appear and reappear at will. It was a body that was not restricted by time or space and could even go through walls. It was a body that still ate and drank.

Reading in the gospels about Jesus after His resurrection demonstrates the power and reality of God. It also shows why the disciples were so convinced that they were even willing to die for this gospel. They were not operating under some illusion but had seen the resurrected Lord with their own eyes. Even Thomas, doubting Thomas, had put his finger into the side of the Lord's resurrected body (John 20:27, KJV). This was where the sword had pierced Him, and Thomas had seen the prints of the nails in His hands and feet (John 20:24-29). After seeing all of this, Thomas exclaimed, *"My Lord and my God." (John 20:28, KJV)* Jesus said to him, *"Thomas, you have believed because you have seen, but more blessed are they who have not seen but yet believed." (John 20:29, KJV).*

According to 1 Corinthians 15, these 11 men, along with hundreds of others, witnessed and saw the resurrected Christ in His glorified body. The Easter story is not just about Him getting up from the dead; it is also about what He did after He got up. It is about the people He saw, the words He said, the places He went, and about the miraculous appearances which were more than convincing to His many followers. This Jesus, who died for our sins, who took our place on that cruel cross, who had done no sins at all, now only asks for our willing obedience so that we can one day enjoy eternal life in heaven with Him.

He desires with great desire to have a relationship with each one of us (Luke 22:15, KJV). Jesus wants to fellowship with His people. Did you not know that this fellowship is possible? Get this, sometimes it seems that what He did after He arose sometimes trumps what He did before He died. As recorded in His word, what

Jesus said and did is likewise forever settled in heaven, whether before or after His resurrection. One thing that He taught us, and that is that for this great relationship with God to be fruitful and multiply, is that we must have a prayer life. We must have an effective prayer life.

What then does prayer do? Prayer secures peace, pardon, and paradise as found in Matthew 7:7, *ask and it shall be given, seek and ye shall find and knock and the door shall be opened unto you.* Jesus also taught us in Luke 18 the importance of being persistent in prayer. A praying saint is a strong saint. A non-praying saint is a weak saint. Even a praying saint can be a weak saint if they are not praying according to God's will and word.

Several stipulations and criteria are spelled out in scripture that will help you develop an effective prayer life. First, David said in Psalm, *"If I regard iniquity in my heart, the Lord will not hear me." (Psalm 66:18, KJV)* Second, Jesus said, *when you stand praying, forgive (Mark 11:25, KJV).* You must get rid of all unforgiveness that may be in your heart against any person. Third, you must *acknowledge Him in all of your ways, and then He will direct your paths (Proverbs 3:5-6, KJV).* Fourth, you should always pray and not faint, and you must *pray without ceasing (1 Thessalonians 5:17, KJV).*

Listen to the widow's parable and the unjust judge and how we are to pattern our prayer life after this persistent woman. She went to the unjust judge (a distinctive contrast with our great and kind heavenly Father) on a continual bug-a-boo basis. She did not care about the talk, the initial rejections, the cruel and mean attitude, and the unjust judge's personality, nor did she care about the time of day. All she knew was that if she were going to be given any fairness or help, this was the only person to whom she could turn and ask. So, she did what a woman in need of special help from the judge had to do. She sent emails, text messages, and she even tweeted him. This lady got on Facebook, mailed numerous amounts of letters, and made phone calls continuously. She even got her friends to assist her in getting the attention of this judge. Why was she going to this extreme? Why was she so persistent? Why did she express her desires to this judge both day and night? Well, she had a need, and there was only one place that she could get help. There was only one place that justice for her could be served. What did the unjust judge finally end up doing for this woman? He avenged her of her adversary. He finally came to her rescue. He finally acted favorably upon her request. This mean, hateful, selfish, egotistical, and self-absorbed man got to the point of disgust, and for himself and his own sake, not hers, he gave in and gave her what she was asking for.

What did Jesus have to say to all of this carrying on by this woman? He did not condemn what she had done. Jesus complimented and commended her for her persistence in asking. *Always pray (1 Thessalonians 5:17, KJV)*. Never cease to pray. Never give up on God and never stop asking. Always keep the lines of communication and open between you and God.

Don't stop praying; the Lord is nigh. He will hear your cry. The Lord has promised, and His word is true. Don't stop praying. He will answer you. Why? Because prayer will fix it for you, prayer is what you should do. Before you give up and let the devil win, go back and pray again. Prayer can sail across the ocean faster than a plane across the sea; prayer can keep your home together; prayer can bring a wandering child back home; prayer can change things, situations, and people. The prayer of faith can raise those that are down. *The prayer of faith will save the sick (James 5:15-16, KJV).* There is deliverance and salvation in the power of prayer. There is healing for the body and the sin-sick soul in the power of prayer.

If you are willing and obedient, you can eat the good of the land (Isiah 1:19, KJV). If you are wondering about getting your prayers answered, He hears us according to His will. I admonish you to get into the secret place and abide under the shadow of the almighty God (Psalm 91:1, KJV). Jesus will never say no. *We walk by faith and not by sight (2 Corinthians 5:7, KJV). We call those things that be not as though they were (Romans 4:17, KJV).* God only needs a clean and pure vessel through whom He wishes to work. He wants to purify and cleanse His bride so that He can use her to bring healing to a dying world (Malachi 3:3, Ephesians 5:26, KJV). *The prayer of faith will save the sick, and the Lord will raise him, and if he has committed sins, they will be forgiven him (James 5:15-16, KJV).*

Others have fallen, but you are still standing. Others have lost their minds, but you are still standing. Others have died with what you are now living with. Your present condition is not your conclusion, and God has not brought you this far just to drop you like a hot potato and leave you alone.

Whatever you do in word or deed, do all in the name of the Lord Jesus (Colossians 3:17, KJV).

Daily Prayer

Father, I am so grateful for the awesome privilege of being able to commune with You. Yes, and truly my fellowship is with the Father and with His Son, Jesus Christ. Oh, how wonderful it is to take everything to God in prayer. I am so blessed to even stand in your presence and not be consumed. Great is thy faithfulness to me. I vow to pray without ceasing and not to faint. Hallelujah, Jesus, I bless Your name. Amen.

CHAPTER 11

Why Was Jesus Manifested

Scripture Reference: 1 John 3:9-13 KJV

We are in the world, but not of this world (John 17:14-16). We talk to people daily, but we do not speak like the world (cussing, joking filthily, lying, and flirting with those other than your spouse, laughing at ungodly comments and jokes). Instead, *our conversation is holy, righteous, and sanctified (1 Peter 1:15, KJV)*—not just in church on Sunday but also daily everywhere we go. We do not become holy when it is convenient for us, but we must remain holy at all times. We sing and enjoy music, but it is not that unholy and degrading music of the world, filthy rap, music that glorifies illicit sex, murder, defies authority, and the like. But instead, our music talks concerning the things of God. We instead make a joyful noise unto the Lord. We dance before Him; we sing songs for Him; we clap hands for Him. We dance the Holy dance, not the provocative and sinful dance moves of the world. We dance for God and God alone (Psalm 100:1, 150:4. KJV). No longer do we shake it for the devil, nor do we drop it like it's hot. We do not even allow ourselves to be caught up like the world. We still dance, but we changed dance partners (we have a new dance partner now; His name is the Holy Ghost). *We are in the world but not of the world (John 17:14-16, KJV).*

The temptation is not to keep it together but to be destroyed by the meaningless of the times. You may not have all that you want materially, but you have all that you need to make it if you have Jesus. Some people depend on the next fix to get them through the next day or two, some are relying on money and their job to help them, some are leaning heavily on their sugar momma and their sugar daddy, some are looking to their parents, and some are looking to their children. How can I cope and how can I go on are questions asked all the time by people everywhere and in every walk of life. They cannot see themselves as being successful or as having accomplished anything so far. But this is a trick from the pits of hell, from the devil himself, and he wants to take away from you your peace of mind and then ultimately land you into a state of depression, anger, frustration, and humiliation. But you must know that the Bible is right when it tells us, *for this reason, was the son of God manifested, that He may destroy the works of the devil (1 John 3:8, KJV).*

Do you remember Job and how he suffered? The devil went and told God that the only reason Job served Him was because God was blessing him so abundantly (Job 1:9-11, KJV). But God had so much confidence in Job that God allowed the devil to attack Job (Job 1:12, KJV). The devil began to have his way with Job and turned him every which way but loose. *From the crown of Job's head to the sole of Job's feet, he was afflicted with sores and boils (Job 2:6-9, KJV).* Job was under mental stress, and his very soul was in anguish. Job was messed up and torn up and was in confusion and delirium. The devil told God that he would make Job curse God to His face (Job 1:11, KJV).

The scripture declares that while Job was under attack from the enemy, after losing his millionaire and wall street status and was homeless, he said *the Lord giveth and the Lord taketh away, blessed be the name of the Lord (Job 1:21, KJV)*. When he saw his body beaten down with sickness, he simply said *though the skin worms destroy my body, yet in my flesh, I will see God (Job 19:26, KJV)*. His wife came to him and told him to curse God and die, but he said no. Job reasoned within himself that if I can curse God and die, I can bless God and live (Job 2:9, KJV). So, what did Job do? He decided to bless God and live. He lived!!!! Job said and declared within himself that *my righteousness I hold fast and will not let it go (Job 27:6, KJV)*. And as Job was determined (God allowed it to be recorded in scripture), we must also be determined. If we hold out, God will prove Himself to be very faithful to us. The devil could not win with Job, so he had to let Job go, and the devil cannot win with you. He will have to let you go. *Now the latter end of Job was better than the first because God blessed him with twice as much as he had lost (Job 42:12, KJV)*. God will give you double for your trouble. Twice as much.

Ollie the Oyster story is an old story that can be like a weathervane for us as used on the top of a rural North Dakota house. This old weathervane points in the right direction and this story about Ollie the Oyster can be used by God to point us, too, in the right direction. Ollie the Oyster was swimming along one day in the ocean, and he was having a wonderful time, with the sun out and the weather warm. He was cruising along at the bottom of the sea happily and joyfully when suddenly, a piece of sand, a piece of ocean grit, got into his skin. That piece of sand hurt so much. Ollie didn't necessarily do anything wrong to get that sand in his life; it just happened. So, Ollie the Oyster cried. He cried and cried, tears and tears, so much so that the ocean slowly rose over the days, weeks, months, and years. Ollie stopped after he had cried for two or three years, and the sand was still there, causing him pain. What to do? Ollie the Oyster started to complain and fuss. He used every complaint in the book that he had ever learned in grade school and junior high school. He complained and complained and complained, so much so that a plume of blue smoke came up from the ocean where he lived.

When Ollie the Oyster was finished complaining, he stopped, and the sand was still there in his side, causing him immense pain. Ollie the Oyster started to pretend. He would pretend that the piece of sand was not in his side. He pretended and pretended and pretended. He suppressed and suppressed and suppressed. When after all those months and years of suppression had passed, he woke up to reality enough to realize the sand was still there, causing him pain. What to do? And slowly, ever so slowly, it began to dawn on Ollie the Oyster. Slowly, oh so slowly, he remembered that he had a special power within, and so he grunted and groaned and groveled, and slowly an excretion of gooey oil came out and surrounded the piece of sand, insulating the sand, and the pain went away.

What a miracle! The pain was gone. And ever so slowly, over time, that gooey substance began to harden around the grain of sand, and in time, it became a pearl. Yes, a pearl, for that is the way that pearls are made. What is the moral of this story? The moral of this story is that we must use the power within us to neutralize the negativity that surrounds us at times. All these negative lies about who we are and who Jesus is. The Holy Ghost is God's power within the believer, which causes them to walk in victory even in trials, tests, tribulations, and even distress. I say this because someone has died with what many of us are living with. Some have lost their minds after having to endure some of the things we have had to endure. We must learn how to use and apply the Holy Ghost power within us to resist temptation and always have gratitude. What is or was your most significant test, temptation, trial that you faced or are having to face? Is it your job, an addiction (alcohol, gambling, or drugs), lying, absolute peril of life's ups and downs? Could it be your marriage or lack thereof? Remember that there is a solution inside every believer that will sustain them in the time most needed. Remember, the Apostle Paul declared that *I can do all things through Christ who strengthens me (Philippians 4:13, KJV).*

Although there are a thousand and one reasons to be sad, choose to obey the word of God, He who gives beauty for ashes, and He who gives the garment of praise for the spirit of heaviness (Isaiah 61:3, KJV).

Daily Prayer

Thank God for Jesus. He is a wonder in my soul. Lord, I have every confidence that You will never leave me nor forsake me. You are on the side of the righteous and will lead me from victory to victory. I confess that I am too blessed to be stressed and too anointed to be disappointed. Yes, Lord, Satan is a defeated foe. Thank You for the victory; I have it now. In Jesus' name, I pray, believe, and receive it. Amen.

CHAPTER 12

Your Gift Is Necessary

Scripture Reference: Joshua 15:13-19 KJV

Your gift is necessary, needful, significant, and purposeful. You are a gift and what God has placed inside you is a gift as well to the body of Christ. Did you not know that God has entrusted you with multiple gifts and talents that He wants you to share with His body? Not only has He entrusted you, but He has equipped you for His service. I want to encourage you to fulfill your God-given purpose. I want you to know that God does not make any junk, and He does not have stepchildren. You are valuable, useful, and have been strategically placed in the body of Christ so that you can be of the most benefit to the kingdom of God. No, you are not an accident, and you are not here by accident. God has brought you here, and that is enough right there for which to give Him praise. The Bible says that *a man's gift makes room for him and brings him before great men (Proverbs 18:16, KJV)*. When used for God, your gifts can potentially have a far and long-reaching effect. Whatever your skill or talent may be, you need to know that it is of absolute value to the Lord's church.

The book of Joshua tells the story of how the Lord allowed the Israelites to conquer and take back possession of the Land of Canaan, commonly referred to as the Promised Land. The chapters in Joshua detail some of the battles and leadership challenges Joshua had to encounter and take on. He was a different leader than his predecessor Moses. Moses was a meek and very tolerant leader, whereas Joshua was a warrior and fighter. He did not play any games and asked no questions. He required obedience and discipline from his soldiers, and he ran a tight ship. Not only that, but he was a spiritual leader and was found often in prayer as he was both asking for and receiving directions from the Lord as to what his next move or task may be.

In Joshua 15, we find Moses' successor begins to fulfill the task of dividing and allotting the territory in the Promised Land to the various tribes and groups of people among the Israelites. This was not an easy task because the land of Israel was not that small. He had to be quite familiar with the land, its borders on all four sides (north, south, east, and west). Of course, he had to be familiar with each mountain, hill, valley, and waterway (rivers, lakes, seas, streams, and tributaries). In Joshua 15, the tribe to be given and allotted land is the Tribe of Judah. Chapter 14 details the land that was allotted to Gad, Rueben, and the half-tribe of Manasseh.

In these chapters, Caleb, Joshua's long-time friend and companion, at 85 years old, was still strong and ready to fight against the sons of Anak, who were the ancestors of Goliath who were not only giants but were very ferocious as well. Caleb requested that Joshua give him the territory and land promised to him by Moses, Mount Hebron, and its associated properties.

Caleb displays his devotion and loyalty to Israel's cause and his commitment to the Lord's servant Joshua. He believed in his leader and was there to support him no matter what the cost. He was a very committed gentleman. He was a very gifted and skilled warrior, and he did not mind using what had been given to him by God for the service of the Lord.

This is what we as people of God must realize. We are gifted, blessed, and highly favored by God to keep our talents for God on display so that we can continue to season the world with our salt and show the world Christ through our light. We were not blessed and favored by God to sit down but are gifted by God to bless others. *Your gift will make room for you (Proverbs 18:16, KJV).* Your gift is necessary.

Caleb has taken on a warrior's task and has a can-do mentality. He does not see his mission as a chore, but instead, he sees it as an opportunity to put God's power on display. He is a man of unusual courage and an undaunting faith in God. Keep working if you are working, get busy working if you are not working, and get back to working for the Lord if you have stopped and decided to give it all up. Your gift is necessary right now.

The Lord used Caleb's gift, his warfighting skills, to defeat, displace and kill the enemy of God's people. That is what you can do with your talent, skills, and abilities. Your job is to confuse and defeat the enemy and to exercise Godly influence to bring those lost souls into the kingdom of God. Your mission is to remain focused and not to become distracted by the cunning craftiness of the devil. You already know that the devil delights in taking us off task, keeping us down in the dumps, and feeling sorry for ourselves. Stay and remain focused on the things of God. Keep your mind stayed on Him. Keep your heart and ways toward Him. Stay on the battlefield and stay on the wall. Build up the body of

Christ by exercising your gifts and talents for the glory of God. The call of God on your life does not always line up with your idea of what success looks like.

If you look at and examine the Apostle Paul's ministry closely, you will say that he undoubtedly had an unsuccessful ministry by modern standards. If you look at Moses and maybe Andrew, Simon Peter's brother, you will say that they had unsuccessful and non-noteworthy ministries. Moses spent 40 years circling the same mountain, and Andrew died a martyr and introduced Simon Peter to Jesus. The Apostle Paul was beheaded, and Peter was crucified upside down. The call of God is not a call to success, but it is a call to faithfulness. He did not call you to be successful, but He did tell you to be faithful. You may never pastor a 400- or 500-member church. You may never possess a million dollars, you may never have a mansion on the hill, or even write a best seller book. But if you are faithful over little, He will make you ruler over much. Although you may not be called successful by modern standards, you are called to be faithful over what the Lord has given you, whether it be little or much.

When we question our success in ministry and see no improvement, it seems, we must ensure that regardless of the result or what it may look like in our human eyes, we must remember that our call is not to succeed, but our call is to faithfulness. Faithful to the choir and music ministry, faithful to your Sunday School class, faithful to your district office, faithful to your job in your local church, faithful to prayer, faithful to the doing of the Word of God, and faithful to the call and gift of God in and on your life. Are you faithful to the call that God has placed on your life? If the answer is yes, you are okay, but you are not okay if your answer is anything other than yes. Be encouraged, pastor, even if the membership is not what you think that it should be. Be encouraged, faithful prayer warrior, even if it seems as if the prayers are not being answered.

After defeating the Sons of Anak, as many as he could in the time allotted, Caleb issues an ultimatum to the 12 tribes of Israel. He promises to reward any successful warrior with his daughter's (Achsah) hand in marriage if they would complete the job that he had started, and that was to finish off and destroy the remaining sons of Anak. There was one brave soul that stepped up; his name is Othinel. Othinel accepted the challenge of using his gifts and Godly influence to defeat the enemy and protect the Israelites (body of Christ) from any further attacks from the enemy of righteousness. Othinel was confident enough in his God-given ability that he just went on and without compromise, without complaint, without thinking twice about it, he just went forth, and God gave him the victory over the rest of those hard-to-get enemies.

We can do all things through Him who gives us victory, ability, and strength (Philippians 4:13, KJV). There is no reason for us not to defeat the enemy (bad habits, drug abuse, fear, poverty, sins in our lives, etc.) because the scripture declares that no man can serve two masters, for you will either hate one and despise the other. *You cannot serve God and the devil simultaneously (Matthew 6:24, KJV).*

After Othinel had defeated those remaining enemies by utilizing his God-given gifts and abilities, Caleb rewarded him with a gift. God is a God of increase and multiplication, a God that keeps His promises. When you are faithful in that which is little, God will make you ruler over many. As you work God's work by using your gifts, God will give you more, and you will be continuously walking in increase.

Why did you stop? *Who or what hindered you (Galatians 5:7, KJV)?* Get back up and start working for the Lord again. Never should you be afraid. You need to stir up the gift (2 Timothy 1:6-7, KJV). God has made room for you because of your unique gifting. You have a special gift, and you know what it is. Begin to go forth in your God-given abilities, and you will be blessed as well as the body of Christ. *Come out from among those who would rather see you defeated in the things of God (2 Corinthians 6:17, KJV).* Come and cast yourself at the Savior's feet. Come and be made complete. He is waiting on you, and you must know that God Loves you.

After their marriage, Achsah asked her husband, Othinel, to visit her father, Caleb. She wanted Othinel to ask Caleb for a better piece of land for both of them. Othinel asked for the land, and Caleb granted his request. But shortly after the conversation between Othinel and Caleb, Achsah (daughter of Caleb and wife of Othinel) shows up riding on a donkey. She dismounts in the presence of both Othinel and Caleb. She is walking toward her dad, no doubt smiling and giving him an unusually kind greeting. He is somewhat surprised and taken aback, and now he knows that this precious gift, his daughter Achsah, is calling for something extra and additional. Your gifts are not to be placed in a bag and put away in some dark God-forsaken place. Many of your God-given talents are hidden, out of sight, and forgotten. Get your talents and let the devil hear loud and clear and see that you will use each of your God-given gifts to and for the glory of God. Consecrate yourself to the point that whatever God chooses to do in your life, you will let Him do it. You will go to the enemy's camp and take back what he has stolen from you. You will not ask nicely for him to give it back, but you will take it back, no questions asked.

Achsah says to her dad that she did not want that land with no water or irrigation. She asked for property that included streams of water in both the northern and southern sectors of her allotted land. She was granted the gift for which she had sought and asked. The scripture says that *if your child asked you for bread, would you give them a stone, or if they asked for clothes, would you give them a scorpion (Luke 11:11, KJV). If you are human beings and are willing to provide good and pleasant gifts to your natural children, how much more will your heavenly Father give the Holy Spirit to them who asks for Him (Luke 11:12, KJV).*

God is trying to bless you. Our God is and always has been in the blessing business, and He wants to bless you, give you additional gifts, and give gifts to those who are already using all the gifts that He has already given them. Get your mindset to get your gifts from God. He may not come when you want Him, but guess what, He is coming. *He that hath begun a good work in you can finish what He started (Philippians 1:6, KJV).*

You can do this because you have a rooted anchor based on two immutable things: *God cannot lie (Numbers 23:19, KJV),* and God keeps His promise, and His Word is steadfast. His Word is steadfast because when God swears or affirms a promise, *He can swear by no greater, so He swears by His name (Hebrews 6:13, KJV).* He has sworn by His name and will indeed keep His promise. Even the scriptures declare in Psalm 138:2 that *God magnifies His Word above His name.* The scripture says *He will not break His covenant, and He will not alter the things that have gone out of His mouth (Psalm 89:34, KJV).* Hebrews declares that our *hope is the anchor for our souls and that anchor is tied securely behind the veil in the holy of holies (Hebrews 6:19, KJV).* You cannot fail, and you will do well as long as you keep hope as the anchor of your soul. Get an anchor hold on the rock that is Christ Jesus, who has by His death, burial, and resurrection given us divine access to the very presence of God in the holy of holies, the place where every promise is fulfilled, and every miracle is wrought. Your gift is necessary and valuable.

Daily Prayer

Thank You, God, that I have been endowed and blessed with spiritual giftings. You, Oh God, have blessed and anointed me on purpose. You have a purpose for my life. I will allow Your purpose and destiny to show up in my life so that others will be blessed through me. Oh, how I love and thank You for choosing me from among so many. In Jesus's name and for His glory, Amen.

CPSIA information can be obtained
at www.ICGtesting.com
Printed in the USA
LVHW081938100222
710546LV00007BA/392

9 781736 445761